Praise for *Bernard Daly's Promise*

"Bernard Daly's remarkable foresight and co   ollege promise for all" has—to this day—enabled thousands of college graduates to succeed in the workforce and in the rest of their lives. Profiled in this extraordinary book, Daly gave us an inspiring legacy that can now be brought to scale for millions more students in every community throughout our nation."

—MARTHA KANTER, CEO, College Promise; US Under Secretary of
   Education (2009–2013)

"Stern weaves together personal narratives and historical statistics to provide rich insights into how Bernard Daly's visionary scholarship affected the life trajectories of families in Lake County. At once historic and timely, local and universal, *Bernard Daly's Promise* provides a novel lens to understand the complex set of forces that shape the American Dream."

—RAJ CHETTY, William A. Ackman professor of economics,
   Harvard University

"*Bernard Daly's Promise* reveals the power of education to transform lives and society. Stern's heart-warming book tells the stories of Daly's visionary philanthropy and its profound impact. Not only does Professor Stern's research uncover individual journeys that resulting from Daly's gift; he also provides the data demonstrating how this act of generosity improved educational outcomes and societal benefits for the region and far beyond."

—SUE CUNNINGHAM, president and CEO, Council for Advancement and
   Support of Education

"Professor Stern tells a uniquely Oregon story about how one man's philanthropy can lift up individuals and communities for a century – and counting. One hundred years after its establishment, the Daly Fund continues to open opportunities to individual students, creating ripple effects in Lake County and far beyond."

—SONIA WORCEL, chief community impact officer, Oregon
   Community Foundation

"A compelling story of philanthropy, opportunity, access to education, and personal journeys. Bernard Daly's scholarship fund was one of the very first place-based scholarships in the nation, when it was established a century ago. Stern has masterfully woven Daly's story into the context of student aid for higher education along with the stories of the scholarship recipients who benefitted from Daly's generosity."
—LARRY LANDIS, former director of Special Collections and Archives,
  Oregon State University

"*Bernard Daly's Promise* is both a page-turner and a work of scholarly importance. Daly personifies the American Dream; his story is an incredible account of the intersection of talent, hard work, and good luck. But the equally fascinating account of the continuing impact of the scholarship he created is truly astonishing. Daly imagined and executed a way to give many hundreds of his fellow Oregonians the chance to develop their minds and characters, and to have the chance to do as much good as their benefactor did. A great read!"
—STANLEY KATZ, professor of Public Policy and International Affairs,
  Princeton University

"In *Bernard Daly's Promise* Sam Stern uncovers a marvelous 100-year-long natural experiment in the benefits of community-based higher education scholarships. This deeply researched book documents the economic and societal returns of the Lake County, Oregon, Daly Fund and engagingly illustrates its life-changing impacts through the stories of beneficiaries. As a bonus, the tale behind the fund is a fun read on its own."
—MICHAEL ETTLINGER, director, Carsey School of Public Policy,
  University of New Hampshire

"A beautifully told story of how one visionary and generous donor's scholarship fund has not only changed the life trajectories of many students from a rural corner of Oregon, but has also catalyzed a community culture that values education for all residents of Lake County. Sam Stern's book is inspirational!"
—ANN C. KUBISCH, president and CEO, The Ford Family Foundation

SAM STERN

BERNARD DALY'S PROMISE

THE ENDURING LEGACY OF A
PLACE-BASED SCHOLARSHIP

OREGON STATE UNIVERSITY PRESS • CORVALLIS
PUBLISHED IN COOPERATION WITH
THE DR. DALY PROJECT

Published in cooperation with the Dr. Daly Project, a Lake County community group with the mission of perpetuating the memory of Dr. Bernard Daly and his scholarship, and the other scholarships modeled after the Daly Scholarship.

Our past educates our future.

Cataloging-in-publication data is available from the Library of Congress.

ISBN 978-0-87071-183-1 (paperback); 978-0-87071-190-9 (ebook)

∞This paper meets the requirements of ANSI/NISO Z39.48-1992 (Permanence of Paper).

First published in 2022 by Oregon State University Press
Printed in the United States of America

Oregon State University Press
121 The Valley Library
Corvallis OR 97331-4501
541-737-3166 • fax 541-737-3170
www.osupress.oregonstate.edu

Dedicated to the people of Lake County

CONTENTS

FOREWORD

Bernard Daly told a high school student that there would be a way for her to go to college someday and realize her dream to become a doctor. That was a big dream in 1918 because she had no financial resources and lived in rural Lake County, Oregon, which was three days' travel from the nearest college and even today has just under eight thousand residents in a county the size of New Jersey. Moreover, less than 2 percent of eighteen- to twenty-four-year-olds in the United States went to college in the early twenties.

But back to the beginning. Bernard Daly was born in Ireland and emigrated to the United States in 1863 with his family to escape the hardship of the Great Potato Famine, which took the lives of one million souls and led two million others to flee, largely to America, reducing the population of Ireland by a fourth, a loss that would not be recovered until the twenty-first century. The family settled in Alabama because northern states such as New York and Massachusetts had passenger laws that kept poor Irish immigrants from entering their ports.

Bernard Daly's Promise is a quick-paced, well-written, and entertaining recounting of a richly lived life and a richer legacy. The first of many wonderful stories is about the life of Bernard Daly, who grew up and became a doctor, banker, county judge, and civic leader in Lake County. His rags-to-riches story is impressive. We learn about the fire that destroyed Lakeview, an unsolved murder, an unrequited love, and a patient who refused to take the doctor's medicine and shot Dr. Daly in the rump. The characters and times come to life in the telling, and this is a wonderful read in itself.

The other stories are reverberations of Daly's extraordinary second act, which began after he passed away in 1920. The creation of the Bernard Daly Educational Fund—and the impact it has had and continues to have on the lives of so many young people from Lake County—is remarkable and heartwarming.

The Daly Fund, established with a million-dollar bequest in 1920, continues to provide at least fifteen Lake County high school graduates each year with four years of financial support for college as long as they keep up their grades and take a full course load. Building on archival material and personal interviews with many Daly scholarship recipients, Sam Stern chronicles their lives and accomplishments. The young lady referred to earlier was one of the first recipients of the Daly Fund Scholarship, and Sam recounts her story among others.

In subsequent decades, others contributed to the Daly Fund and created complementary funds in Lake County. Nationally, a number of people have recently created promise scholarship programs for schools and communities to encourage young people to go to college and realize their full potential. Bernard Daly was a hundred years ahead of his time. Clearly, he believed as Sam and I do that our graduates are our most important contribution to the future. What an extraordinary second act. These are wonderful, inspiring stories.

Ed Ray, President Emeritus and Professor of Economics,
Oregon State University

INTRODUCTION

It's a strong memory. My family lived in Detroit, and I was probably seven or eight at the time. I was with my dad, and we were driving somewhere in the city on a bitter-cold winter day. On a corner with a White Castle hamburger shop, I saw a large gathering of men just standing around. I asked my dad why they were standing outside on such a cold day. He told me they were day laborers, waiting in the hope that someone would stop and pick them up for a day's work. I asked, "Why did they decide to do that?" I was young and naive; I simply thought one decided what to do in life and did it. I didn't yet know that choices are constrained, much more for some than others. I was fortunate in that my parents were each the first in their family to go to college, and their careers in education gave me an insider's advantage. Not all are so fortunate. Many don't have parents who went to college and found success, and some are quite distant from higher education and the advantages it grants.

It is hard to imagine a place more distant from higher education than Lake County, Oregon. In south central Oregon, Lake County is about the same geographic size as the state of New Jersey but with a much smaller population of just under eight thousand—more than a square mile per person. A hundred years ago, when the Bernard Daly Scholarship was first awarded in 1922, less than 2 percent of America's eighteen- to twenty-four-year-olds went to college. Public colleges were relatively new, a long way from the established institutions of today. Oregon had only three state colleges: Oregon Agricultural College (today's Oregon State University), University of Oregon, and Oregon Normal School (today's Western Oregon University), all struggling to attract students. The state colleges were far from Lakeview, the largest town in Lake County. The closest college, the University of Oregon, was a three-day trip by horse, ferry, and train. Not surprisingly, only a few Lake County students went to college.

That changed forever in 1922 when Bernard Daly established a scholarship fund that made it possible for Lake County students to attend college. Since then, most of the high school graduates from that remote county have gone on to college and remarkable careers. It's an improbable and truly remarkable story that began with an immigrant seeking a better life.

Fleeing the aftermath of the Irish Potato Famine, five-year-old Bernard Daly and his family managed to get through the Union blockade in the midst of the Civil War to settle in Alabama. Somehow he found his way to college and then medical school at a time when few went to college, and those who did were privileged and wealthy, not poor immigrants. Settling in the newly established town of Lakeview, he was the town doctor and went on to become a successful rancher, banker, state legislator, and county judge. He never married, and when he died in 1920, he left an estate worth about a million dollars, almost all of which he dedicated to creating a college scholarship fund for the youth of Lake County.

At a time when almost no one went to college, Daly created a college-for-all possibility in that remote corner of America. Just imagine if someone said, "Let's pick a remote rural community and provide funds so that most of the youth in the community can go to college, and let's do it every year for a hundred years, and then go back and see what happened."

Well, it did happen, and this book tells the story—the story of Bernard Daly and the recipients of his scholarship. Most importantly, it is a story of great generosity and the returns of that generosity.

I first learned about the Daly Fund forty years ago, shortly after I joined the faculty in the College of Education at Oregon State University (OSU). My friend and OSU colleague Dan Dunham (LHS, 1954) told me that he grew up in Lakeview and was a scholarship recipient. Dan's story stuck with me. Later, our college newsletter profiled three sisters—Sue Ogle Densmore (LHS, 1967), Martha Ogle Powell (LHS, 1971), and Sara Ogle Lea (LHS, 1976)—all of whom received the scholarship and went to OSU. I began to think about a research project that would look at the long-term impact of the Daly Fund. It was a natural experiment just waiting to be studied.

But the research would have to wait thirty years until I was close to retirement. As I neared the end of my time as dean of the OSU College of Education and had the time to pursue the project, I went to Lakeview and met first with Jim Lynch (LHS, 1954), the longtime secretary-treasurer of the Daly Fund, and then with several of the trustees and scholarship recipients. I was hooked! Since that visit, I've been on a journey of discovery, learning about the remarkable life of Bernard Daly, the many people his scholarship impacted, and Lake County, the place where this story started.

My journey began with a list of scholarship recipients for each year since 1922—about two thousand names in total—no addresses, no contact information at all, and, to make things even more complicated, most of the women's names had changed with marriage. And, since educational level is highly correlated with mobility, most of the recipients had moved far from Lake County. How would I find them?

As I started with those still living in Lake County, I began to learn the whereabouts of others, then created a community Facebook page for the project. It grew as one person shared it with another, then both Oregon State University and the University of Oregon helped by cross-referencing my list of scholarship recipients with their alumni lists. Finally, I had found enough recipients in 2016 for a web-based survey that revealed the remarkable impact of the Fund.

To better understand that impact, I interviewed scholarship recipients as well as those who didn't get the scholarship, ranging from high school graduates about to begin college to a ninety-nine-year-old who graduated from Lakeview High School in 1936. Through the survey and the interviews, I learned much about the educational, economic, and social impacts of the Daly Fund. The impact was, and still is, huge.

Consider the example of Cornelia (Connie) Robertson, who was among the first group of students to receive the scholarship in 1922. She told a reporter from the *Oregon Journal* about how she would talk with Dr. Daly at the telegraph office where she worked while he waited for the night rates to go into effect. "He was always buying and selling cattle and sheep. A lot of people didn't think he had a lick of money, I know." When the doctor asked what she planned to do with her life, she replied "I'd like to study medicine, but I don't think my father can afford it." Daly replied, "Don't worry. There'll be a way."[1] Daly died a year later, and two years after that, Connie left for college, then to medical school, and on to a career as a doctor, first in New York City, then San Diego, and finally Lakeview. More about Connie in chapter 4.

Given that the Daly Fund provides a four-year scholarship, one would expect educational impact for the students themselves, but the impact is even greater than might be imagined. Consider the graduation rate and time to graduation. An especially important indicator for higher education is the six-year graduation rate, a measure of how many students who began in the same cohort will graduate from a four-year program in six years. The six-year graduation rate for first-time, full-time undergraduate students who began seeking a bachelor's degrees at US public four-year degree-granting institutions in fall of 2012 was 62 percent. At Oregon's two major public universities, Oregon State University and the University of Oregon, it was about 70 percent during the same time period.

Our survey showed that more than 90 percent of Daly Fund recipients graduated in six years or less. Even more surprisingly, about 70 percent of the survey respondents completed their degrees in four years, almost double the national and state averages of about 39 percent. To put it another way, more Daly scholarship students completed their degrees in four years than the overall percentage of US college students who graduated in six years.

Many benefits are associated with timely completion of a college degree. It reduces the cost of higher education to the student, the university, and the public; it also maximizes the returns. From a cost standpoint, completing a degree in six years rather than four is considerably more costly when one considers the value of foregone income in those extra two years. From an educational standpoint, students who complete undergraduate degrees without assuming debt are far more likely to earn graduate and professional degrees, as Connie did so many years ago.

So it is not surprising that a great many Lake County youth go on to complete graduate and professional degrees. While about 12 percent of the general US population have graduate degrees, more than three times as many (40 percent) of the survey respondents have either a master's or an advanced professional degree. The high percentage of students earning advanced degrees was likely influenced by completing their bachelor's degrees early and the fact that they graduated with little or no debt, giving them both time and money to invest in further education. As you will learn in the chapters to come, a great many Lake County graduates went on to successful careers.

Bernard Daly, known for being frugal and fiscally conservative, would have been quite pleased with the economic return associated with the scholarship he created. It was a good investment.Most of the scholarship recipients finished college without assuming debt, and those who did reported relatively small amounts. Though the number of Daly scholarship recipients reporting debt increased over time as the cost of college increased, the percentage with debt and the amount borrowed were still considerably less than the national average in 2019, when college graduates reported an average debt of more than $30,000.

The scholarship itself minimizes the need for debt as it continues to provide about a third of the estimated total cost of college for four consecutive years as long as the recipients maintain the required grade point average and full-time enrollment. As you will learn from the recipients themselves in the chapters to come, the amount of the scholarship support was enough for them to make up the difference through a combination of careful money management and work, both of which are certainly good life values that would serve the students well in their future lives.

The economic returns continued as Daly scholarship recipients left college and began their careers. Almost all of the survey respondents reported that the Daly Fund had some or great impact on their economic circumstances. When asked about their most recent annual household income, about half reported annual incomes greater than $100,000, and a quarter reported annual incomes greater than $150,000–almost five times greater than the median annual household income in Lake County of about $33,000. The high annual household incomes Daly scholarship recipients reported are largely due to their high levels of education (over 90 percent have bachelor's degrees, and more than 40 percent hold graduate degrees) rather than previous family wealth. When asked how their income compared to that of their parents, about three-quarters reported that their family income was either somewhat or much more than that of their parents when they were growing up. The Daly Fund has been providing opportunity for upward financial mobility–an "American Dream Machine," fulfilling the promise of the American Dream that has become less realistic for many youth.

In addition to educational and economic gains, the scholarship has also led to greater philanthropy, serving as a catalyst for community engagement and charitable giving. Recipients of the Daly scholarship have made contributions to the Fund and have created additional scholarships for Lake County youth and others. Lake County has more endowed funds to support higher education than any other county in America.

The bottom line is that Lake County college graduates are much more likely to go to college, graduate in four years without debt, and go on to graduate and professional school, have successful careers, and contribute to the larger community–all because of a scholarship established a hundred years ago by an immigrant who sought a better life, not only for himself but also for others.

Tracking Bernard Daly's path from Ireland to Selma and then to Lakeview also proved challenging. With the help of historic and genealogical records and especially his correspondence with Pearl Hall (much more about her and their relationship later in the book), I was able to piece together the story of his journey.

Daly's life was buffeted by great, often tragic, world events, yet he thrived and did much to improve the situation wherever he lived. He arrived in Lakeview just ten years after the small town was established. He became the town doctor, member and chair of the school board, banker, rancher, state senator, county judge, and a regent of Oregon Agricultural College (today's Oregon State University). Although he held many prominent positions, he lived modestly in a boarding house and developed a reputation for being especially frugal. According to local accounts, he rarely bought new clothing and seemed to subsist on an occasional nickel bowl of soup and a handful of crackers.

Daly's frugality allowed him to fulfill his promise to Connie Robertson—and to all youth of Lake County—through his will, in which he wrote:

> It is my earnest desire to help, aid and assist worthy and ambitious young men and women of my beloved county of Lake, to acquire a good education, so that they may be the better fitted and qualified to appreciate and help to preserve the laws and constitution of this free country, defend its flag, and by their conduct as good citizens reflect honor on Lake County and the State Oregon.

CHAPTER 1

AN IMMIGRANT COMES TO AMERICA (1863–1887)

Out of Ireland into the heart of the Confederacy. Carrying
hods in the Bronx. Going to college at Ohio Normal.
Becoming a doctor. Heading west to find his fortune.

Much of Bernard Daly's life seems to have happened despite great odds. His family was one of a great many who left Ireland after the Great Famine. Recognized as the greatest humanitarian disaster of nineteenth-century Europe, it resulted in the Irish population shrinking by almost a third, with more than a million deaths and about two million who left the country.

He was only five years old when his family emigrated to Selma, Alabama, at the end of the Civil War, a time when all immigration to the United States had practically stopped. Though there were few legal limits to migration at the time (passports and visas were not yet required), the greatest barriers were inertia and lack of money: people do not want to move away from family and friends, and it takes resources to relocate. Those who emigrate do so for a strong reason, often when their lives, livelihood, or liberty are threatened. And so it was for Bernard Daly and his family, who left the poverty of Ireland for the promise of a new life in America.

Little is known of Daly's life in Ireland, but it certainly must have been hard. He was born on February 17, 1858, in Northern Ireland. Many accounts report that he was born in County Mayo, where the Famine was particularly bad; nearly 90 percent of the population depended on the potato crop for their sustenance. In the aftermath of the Famine, the county experienced the highest level of emigration out of Ireland. In *The Graves are Walking*, John Kelly wrote, "In Mayo, something like outright anarchy developed. Deaths innumerable from starvation; plunder, robberies, occurring every day. The bonds of society almost dissolved."[1]

Although the Famine was at its worst in the 1840s, poverty persisted for years. From the 1840s through the 1880s, waves of emigrants left Ireland in search of a better life—millions to the United States. Between 1820 and 1860, the Irish constituted over a third of all US immigrants. While the poorest of the poor in Ireland could not afford the passage, many of those who could were still poor and, because of the long voyage, were often in bad health when they arrived. They were different than most Americans of the time. Many were Catholic, did not speak English, and lacked job skills. When times were good, they were welcomed as cheap labor; when times were bad, as they were in the 1850s, the Irish suffered discrimination. Job postings often included the phrase, "No Irish need apply." Anti-immigrant feelings grew, leading to the emergence of the country's first anti-immigrant political party, the Know Nothing Party. *

It was in those times that New York and Massachusetts, home to the nation's busiest ports, implemented state passenger laws specifically intended to keep poor Irish out. These laws required ship captains to post bonds that would cover the costs of maintaining indigent passengers at charitable institutions and, in some cases, send them back to their country of origin.[2] These state passenger laws were our country's first immigration laws and it is likely they are the reason Bernard Daly and his family emigrated to Selma, Alabama.

Why would Daly's family emigrate from Ireland to Selma, Alabama, toward the end of the Civil War? Entering through the nearby port of Mobile, Alabama, may very well have been the best option available to them at the time. With major northern seaboard ports effectively closed to poor Irish at the time, the remaining (and risky) options were the Confederate ports of the South. One by one, the Union blockaded the Confederate ports, and after the fall of New Orleans in 1862, Mobile was the Confederacy's premier cotton port and leading destination for Confederate blockade runners. It is likely that Daly and his family were on one of the British ships that ran the blockade of Mobile. Great Britain and Ireland were neutral during the Civil War, but English speculators financed

---

*A secret society known as the Order of the Star Spangled Banner with initiation rites, memorized passwords and hand signals, and a solemn pledge never to betray the order. Members were not allowed to talk about the secret society. If asked, they would respond by saying, "I know nothing." The Know Nothing Party reached its peak in the 1850s while advocating for the deportation of foreign beggars, a twenty-one-year naturalization period for immigrants, mandatory Bible reading in schools, and elimination of all Catholics from public office.

blockade runners who brought munitions and some passengers to the South and cotton back to Britain. When the Daly family stepped off the boat in Mobile, the city was known as the Paris of the Confederacy; a quarter of its population were foreigners who enjoyed the city's many coffee houses, oyster bars, beer and wine shops, gambling houses, and dance halls.[3]

Selma, only a hundred and fifty miles from Mobile, was the center of the Confederate's military manufacturing, producing tons of supplies, munitions, and warships. It is likely that Daly's parents were among the more than ten thousand people who worked there. Not much is known about the Daly family's time in Selma or even how long they lived there. Bernard's earliest experiences with school would have been in Selma at the end of the Civil War and then during Reconstruction era.

Very little would be known about Bernard Daly's life before his arrival in Lakeview in 1887 if it were not for Pearl Hall. Several years after his arrival in Lakeview, Bernard met Pearl, who was the sister of his friend Thomas Vinton Hall. Daly was quite taken with her, and shortly after their meeting, a long and loving relationship developed. Though they would never marry, the relationship would last the rest of his life. Pearl saved many of the letters Bernard wrote to her and other materials, including her notes for a book about Daly that she never completed. After her death in 1956, these materials were given to the University of Oregon Archives Special Collections.

In her notes, Pearl wrote that from an early age, Bernard was ambitious and wanted an education. After his parents died when he was very young, his brothers and sisters looked out for him. He had five older siblings: three brothers—Tom, James, and Hugh—and two sisters—Mary Alice and Margaret. For a time, he lived with his brother Hugh, who was a contractor in the Bronx, New York. Bernard helped at whatever he was able to do, and, as he told Pearl, he worked hard as a young boy carrying hods—three-sided boxes with long handles used to carry bricks, mortar, and other building materials for the builders. New York was not Bernard Daly's only stop after Selma. Sometime later, he found his way to Texas and then to Ohio, where his sister Mary Alice Daly Mullen lived.

In the fall of 1883, Daly began studies at Ohio Normal University (today's Ohio Northern University) in Ada, Ohio.[4] Ohio Normal was established in 1871 by twenty-seven-year-old Henry Solomon Lehr, who was the popular town schoolmaster in Ada. Since 1866, he had been teaching more challenging classes to interested townspeople in the evenings. By 1870, his evening classes had become so popular that Lehr was able to convince Ada residents to help finance his college. Northwestern Ohio was still considered a frontier area, and the townspeople hoped that the college would lead to more settlers.

During the two or three decades following the Civil War, private academies and private normal schools* provided much of the teacher training that was in demand, in part because of the growing common school movement, which established free public education for primary grades. But it was not long before state-supported normal schools were established throughout the country to meet the need for teacher preparation. Ohio Normal was one of the few private normal colleges that lasted beyond the lifetime of its founder and successfully morphed into a full-fledged university offering degrees in many fields.

At first, Lehr's new college focused on the needs of teachers. Most school-teachers of the time had only an elementary education; with the push for common schooling through the eighth grade, they needed more advanced instruction to stay at least a step ahead of their students. Ohio Normal began in 1871 with an enrollment of 131, but during the winter term when teachers left to return to their schools, enrollment dropped to only 40 students. Lehr had to mortgage his home to make the payments on the loan the townspeople made for the school. He also took on new partner investors and began to offer different fields of study.[5]

When Bernard Daly first enrolled in 1883, enrollment had grown to 2,062, and students could enroll in the literary course, scientific course, classical course, or the more general university course.** According to Ohio Normal records, Daly enrolled in the scientific course, which at the time included classes in both science and civil engineering. It seems Daly was attracted to Ohio Normal because of its intent to establish a medical program. In 1882, the year before Daly enrolled, a preparatory medical program was established and courses in anatomy and physiology were offered as well as some preliminary work in dissection. As described in the *Ada Record*, "The physiology classes of the university are doing a good work in ridding [the] town of worthless curs

---

*Normal schools were established in the 1800s to prepare teachers in the "norms" of pedagogy and curriculum. Most normal schools were public colleges, many of which have become more comprehensive universities.

**Lehr and his small faculty were quite entrepreneurial, offering other areas of instruction for additional fees: architecture for an additional $25 per term, stenography for $8, telegraphy for $30, law for $30 a year, and pharmacy for $15 a term.

which they use as subjects for anatomical demonstrations."[6] Given the institution's meager resources, it is not surprising that the medical program failed to develop, progressing only to the point of buying a skeleton.

According to Pearl Hall's notes, Daly's sister Mary Alice and her husband claimed to have financed Bernard's college costs. Their son, Bernard's nephew, told Pearl Hall that Bernard borrowed the money and was expected to pay it back, but both of his parents died before Daly graduated. The nephew may have been motivated to make the claim because he was the only nephew or niece overlooked in Daly's will. In any case, Daly did have the money to attend Ohio Normal. According to the 1885 catalog, the tuition was eight dollars for each ten-week term, and room and board in a local private home cost from $2.50 to $3.00 per week, about three times the cost of tuition. The comparison of tuition and rooming costs over time shows the very large increase in tuition costs since those early days. Today, more than a century after Daly attended college, it is typical for tuition and fees at a publicly supported college to be two or three times the cost of campus housing; at a private college, it may be as much as four to five times greater.

In 1941, Pearl Hall traveled to Ada, Ohio, to learn about Daly's college days. While there, she met Sarah Lehr Kennedy, the daughter of Henry Lehr, founder of the college and president while Daly was a student. Sarah recalled a time when Daly had come to take her to the college where she was to perform. Though she was only twelve at the time, she remembered that he wore a green wooly suit and that he had perfect manners. She thought he was French. *

Based on interviews with some of Bernard's classmates, Pearl wrote this in her notes:

> His classmates remarked upon Bernard Daly's courtesy and polite manners toward everyone. Each person I contacted said Bernard Daly was well liked and a hardworking student, that he had money and never borrowed neither did he ever talk of his childhood, his family or himself—very reticent—not that he had anything to be reticent about but that was his nature always concerning his past life and his achievements.[7]

---

*Young Sarah was partly right. In the 1900 census, Bernard Daly identified his father as being Irish and his mother, French.

It does seem that Daly was a good student. He earned high grades in all subjects and in his last year taught the college anatomy class. Given that Daly completed his degree in less than three years, it is likely he obtained credit for many classes through exams, an indication that he was well prepared for college studies.

Daly was also active in the college student literary societies, which were such an important part of campus life in those days. The societies were independent student-run organizations that fostered competition within and between the societies through debates and public speaking. They were the training grounds for men in public affairs in the nineteenth century. As a student at Mount Union College in Alliance, Ohio, Henry Lehr was a member of a literary society; as a new teacher in Ada, he required that his students be members of the Ciceronian literary society. At first it was not popular, especially among the boys. However, gradually they joined in the debates, wrote essays, and created a humorous society paper. Community members began to come to society meetings to hear the debates and orations, some from as far as twenty miles away. Realizing the importance of these societies to learning, Lehr wanted to institute them at Ohio Normal but thought it would be better to have two competing societies. On the first Friday night of the first term of the new college, Lehr called the roll, with students being alternately assigned as a member of either the Franklin Society or the Philomathean Society. Daly became a "Philo," and it proved to be an important part of his college experience. A decade after his graduation, Daly responded to an alumni survey that included the question, "What studies of work have you found to be most beneficial?" His answer was "literary work in society." His participation in the Philos, with the discussions and debates of controversial issues not covered in the school curricula, was excellent preparation for his future of public service.[8]

At his commencement ceremony in July 1886, Daly was one of the salutatory speakers. According to the commencement program, he spoke about medical science.[9] Shortly after graduation, the *University Herald*, a monthly review of the school and societies, included this entry:

> Bernard Daly is missed at Ada by his many friends having gone to
> Louisville, Ky., where he will graduate in the spring and come out
> a full-fledged M.D. – He is making things boom down there on the

border land of Dixie and bids fare to stand as high in the estimation of
Louisville people as he does at Ada. Before leaving he presented the
Philos with three books and five dollars in cash.[10]

Disappointed that Ohio Normal did not offer a medical program, Daly enrolled
in the University of Louisville Medical Department. In the late 1800s, Louisville
was a center of medical education. During the years Daly was in Louisville, there
were eight medical schools with a total of about fifteen hundred medical students in a city with a population of just under two hundred thousand. There were
so many medical students at the time that it was common to classify the city's
residents in four categories: white persons, colored persons, dogs, and medical
students, in descending order of social acceptability.[11]

The largest and most highly regarded of the Louisville medical schools was
the University of Louisville medical program. Like other medical programs of
the time, it began as a proprietary school, operated as a commercial enterprise
by successful area physicians to supplement their income. In the mid-1800s, the
program became a part of the newly established University of Louisville. When
Daly arrived in 1886, the college was slowly moving toward more full-time faculty and a curriculum that reflected emerging national standards.[12]

Once again, Daly found himself on the verge of a major change; in this case,
it was the medical profession that was changing. At the time, medical education
was transitioning from informal apprenticeship to professional university-based
education. In the nineteenth century, most medical education happened through
an apprenticeship with an experienced doctor or at a proprietary school owned
by local physicians. Relatively few doctors had attended university medical programs, and those programs were highly variable in their admissions requirements, curriculum, and length. There was no standard for a medical degree.[13]

Shortly after Daly graduated, the American Medical Association created the
Council on Medical Education with the objective of restructuring medical education. The Council turned to the Carnegie Foundation for the Advancement of
Teaching, whose president picked Abraham Flexner to lead a nationwide survey
of the state of medical education. This was an unusual choice as Flexner was not
a physician, scientist, or medical educator; in fact, he had never set foot in a medical school. He did have a bachelor's degree from the University of Louisville;
operated a for-profit school in Louisville, Kentucky; and, more to the point, had

just written a book, *American College*, in which he criticized the traditional lecture approach that seemed to make up the entirety of college instruction.[14] One of Flexner's only connections to medicine was through his brother Simon, who graduated from the University of Louisville medical school in 1889, just two years after Daly. After serving as the first director of the Rockefeller Institute for Medical Research, Simon Flexner went on to a distinguished medical career.

With astonishing energy, Abraham Flexner visited all 155 medical programs in the United States. He was harshly critical of almost all of them, especially those proprietary schools that were primarily commercial enterprises. Two of Flexner's recommendations were that medical education should last at least six and preferably eight years and that it adhere closely to the scientific method and be thoroughly grounded in human physiology and biochemistry. The gap between Flexner's ideal medical program and existing programs was enormous. Following the report, more than half of all American medical schools closed or merged; those that remained closely followed the guidelines outlined in what is commonly referred to as the Flexner Report.[15]

The Flexner Report contained profiles on every medical school along with an evaluation of how far they were from Flexner's ideal program. The entry for the University of Louisville program, based on Flexner's 1909 visit, found that entrance requirements were highly variable, with some students admitted from two-year high schools. At the time of the visit, there were a total of six hundred students and ninety teaching staff. Flexner, who was critical of programs that relied exclusively on lectures, reported that the University of Louisville program had an affiliation with the city hospital, where students completed clinical practice; however, he found the hospital facilities to be poor and unequal to the task of preparing even a smaller body of students, let alone what he described as the largest medical school enrollment in the country.[16]

Daly attended the University of Louisville in 1886 and 1887, about a decade before Flexner's visit, but the entry is likely to be a good description of Daly's experience. Daly's medical education consisted of only two semesters of classes, including lecture-based classes and clinical instruction at the hospital. Although far from the ideal of six to eight years, Daly's formal preparation was more than most doctors at the time received. At his graduation in June 1887, Daly was recognized as one of the top ten graduates among a graduating class of about a hundred.

At twenty-nine years of age and already well traveled, Daly headed west as did so many in those days. The relatively new transcontinental rail lines brought him to northern California, and then a horse-drawn stage took him to Lakeview, Oregon.

When he first arrived in Lakeview, it was a small community with a population of about three hundred, located more than 150 miles from the nearest railroad. The town residents were self-reliant in most respects, but they needed a town doctor. So, when Daly arrived, threadbare and practically broke, the residents were thrilled and encouraged him to stay. And stay he did.

CHAPTER 2

EARLY YEARS IN LAKEVIEW
1887–1900

*Stepping off the stagecoach. An early town leader. Oregon's
first state colleges. A term in the state legislature and a most
unusual term as state senator. The life of a country doctor.
Daly's heroism in one of Oregon's worst catastrophes.
Becoming a banker and a rancher.*

When Daly arrived in the horse-drawn stage that brought him from Klamath
Falls to Lakeview, the first person he met was Frank Light. Mr. Hopkins, the
proprietor of the Hopkins Hotel, which also served as the stage depot, had asked
Light to meet Daly, as he would be a guest at the hotel. As it turned out, Light
and Daly became close friends. They both lived at the Hopkins Hotel for a time,
and even after Light married and moved out of the hotel, he and Daly had breakfast together most mornings.

Light recalled a conversation with Mr. Hopkins shortly after Daly arrived in
town. The arrival of a doctor in the newly established frontier town was big news.
Hopkins and Light agreed that it would be good if the new arrival liked the area
and was able to withstand the hardships that came with being a doctor in such a
remote community. Then it would be important for the people of the community
to like him—they certainly wouldn't take to any "city dude."

According to Light's account, Mr. Hopkins often joked with Daly about doctors. He was known to say, "You doctors are all alike. After you prescribe for a
man until you get all of his money, you then tell him to go below. That is always
the last prescription." In Lakeview, the term go below referred to a trip to San
Francisco, which is where people went to see a medical specialist when they were
seriously ill. So it was a play on words—a bit of black humor equating a trip to San
Francisco with burial. As it would turn out, the story proved all too prophetic in
Daly's own case.[1]

Daly arrived in Lakeview just as it was emerging from its pioneer ways. Settlers on their way west stopped and often stayed. Through the 1880s, the town grew steadily to reach a population of about three hundred in 1887. Two years later, the citizens of Lakeview sought a charter from the state to be recognized as an incorporated town. The act incorporating Lakeview became law on February 20, 1889, requiring the newly incorporated town be governed by an elected mayor and council of four members.

Daly had arrived at a critical juncture, just as the town of Lakeview was about to be formed, and it is easy to understand why he became one of the town's first leaders. As the local doctor, he was one of very few professionals in the area, and probably one of very few who had gone to college. At the time, only about two percent of all students in the country went to high school.[2] In a place as remote as Lakeview, the percentage would have been even lower.

Public colleges in the late 1800s were very much like a start-up enterprise of today. Their initial funding came from federal land grants provided by the Morrill Land Grant Act of 1862 and modest state appropriations. With the secession of the Confederate states and their congressional representatives who were opposed to the Morrill Act, it passed along with two companion pieces of legislation: the Homestead Act and the Pacific Railroad Act, which promoted the construction of the transcontinental railroad. Together these acts were intended to develop the western states and promote education for more people by establishing a new type of college.[3]

Along with the land grants of thirty thousand acres for every senator and congressman came the requirement that the new college would "teach such tactics as are related to agriculture and the mechanic arts . . . to promote the liberal and practical education of the industrial classes in the several pursuits and professions of life." Contrasted with more established private colleges of the time that focused on the study of classics, these were practical—colleges for the people. Because of their importance to agriculture, most of the land-grant colleges were located in rural areas. Oregon's land-grant college, Oregon Agricultural College, was located in Corvallis in the middle of the fertile Willamette Valley, about three hundred miles northwest of Lakeview.

About a decade later, in 1876, the Oregon State Legislature decided to take advantage of a clause in the Statehood Act that provided seventy-two sections of public land to support the creation of a state university. Designated the

University of Oregon, it was located in Eugene, just forty-five miles south of Corvallis. In those early years, both struggled to survive, and as is the situation in many other states, the two major state colleges developed a rivalry and ongoing competitive tension.

In 1870, 169 students were enrolled at Oregon Agricultural College, but only 28 were at the college level; the majority were enrolled in high school college preparatory classes. In 1880, the Oregon Commissioner of Education reported that the University of Oregon, established a few years earlier in 1876, offered 113 free scholarships, one for each county and one for each member of the legislative assembly. At the time, the total college enrollment was 114; it seems as if one student attended without having been nominated for a scholarship. Neither of the state colleges would have survived if not for the students enrolled in the college-preparatory programs.[4]

As someone who had gone to college and to medical school, Daly must have stood out in the community. It is not surprising that he was elected as one of four town council members and also as a member of the newly formed school board. He went on to serve in elected or appointed positions for the remainder of his life. His particular interest in education was clear from the beginning as he served continuously on the school board for thirty years.

Daly's election to the Oregon House in 1892, representing Lake, Crook,* and Klamath counties, is an indication of how well-known he had become since arriving in the area just five years earlier. A lifelong Democrat in a strong Republican region, Daly won the three-county election with what the 1894 *Oregonian's Handbook* described as a "most flattering majority."[5] At that time, the legislature only met in odd years for about forty days, starting in early January. Members were truly citizen legislators in that they all had jobs outside of their legislative work.

A reading of the *Journal of the Oregon House* for 1893 shows Daly to have been an engaged representative. He was rarely absent and often made motions and amendments. Daly served as chair of the medicine and pharmacy committee. In addition to showing interest in legislation related to his district, he was also involved in matters related to finance and education. On the last day of the

---

*At that time, Crook County covered all of central Oregon, including what are now Deschutes and Jefferson counties.

legislative session, the Committee on Salaries and Mileage reported on the mileage and reimbursement for each representative. Daly, with 1,896 miles, reimbursed at fifteen cents per mile, had traveled the most of any member.[6]

Another sign of Daly's growing stature was his appointment to the Oregon Agricultural College Board of Regents in 1893. Governor Pennoyer, one of two Populist governors in US history, appointed Daly, a Democrat, to replace the Republican William Ladd, who had long served as president of the Board of Regents.

Daly's journeys to Salem when he served in the legislature and to Corvallis for meetings of the college regents were more like an endurance test than a trip. A horse-drawn stage left Hopkins House in Lakeview between six and seven in the evening. Traveling through the night, the stage was able to reach Bly in time for breakfast. By noon, it was at Bonanza for lunch, then on to Klamath Falls for supper. After allowing only a half hour for the stop, the stage continued on to Ager, in northern California, where Daly caught the train north toward Ashland, Salem, and Portland. There was a particularly bad section of road between Shovel Creek and Ager where Daly and the other passengers had to walk and help push the stage along. From the time he left Hopkins House to his arrival at the state capital in Salem was a three-day trip.

Travel was certainly part of the job of a country doctor in a county the size of New Jersey. Daly was known for his willingness to go anywhere by any means available to help the sick or injured. A newspaper article in the *Lake County Examiner* after his death described the travel and hardships associated with his practice:

> Many were the fearful night rides he was called upon to make, and numerous instances are related where he seemed to be possessed of almost superhuman endurance during his younger days. No instance is known where he refused to answer a call although he might have just returned from a long tiresome trip extending over several days and nights. His record as a physician in relieving the suffering and answering the call of his afflicted is doubtless without parallel in the annals of the Northwest, if not the whole world.[7]

Despite this claim that he would go anywhere and never refused to answer a call for help, there is one story about a time he did refuse to treat someone. Warner

"Buck" Snider,* Lake County Sheriff in the early 1900s, enjoyed telling the story of Daly and a locally known "two-gun bad man" called Long John. It seems that Long John was in town giving a local saloon bartender a hard time until the bartender pulled out a snub-nosed .38 and shot Long John in the chest. Long John fell to the floor, and the bartender ran to the courthouse, where Snider was on duty. Snider went to get Daly, who was asleep in bed. While getting dressed, Daly asked the identity of the patient. When Snider told him it was Long John, Daly got back in bed and refused to go. He told Snider that he had once gone to a local hotel to treat Long John, who was sick. Long John refused to take any of the medicine Daly prescribed or do anything the doctor told him, so Daly closed his bag, headed for the door, and told Long John to just lie there and die. Long John pulled a pistol from under his pillow and shot Daly in the rump.

Snider returned to the saloon, where he found Long John lying full length on a pool table. Snider couldn't find any evidence of blood but did see lumps on Long John's chest. It seemed that the bullets had gotten caught in his woolen underwear and had not pierced his skin. When Long John realized he was not wounded, just bruised and stunned, he rolled off the table, ran out the door to his horse, and was never seen in Lakeview again.

Like other country doctors of the time, Daly was called to treat a wide variety of ailments, including gunshot wounds but also farming accidents, fevers, heart disease, toothaches, and even sick livestock. Since Daly had to travel considerable distances, he typically treated patients in their homes with only the medical tools and drugs he could carry on horseback. Even so, Daly was better equipped than most. He was one of the few who had gone to medical school and knew about germ theory and the use of anesthesia during surgery. Until the later 1800s and the advent of medical licensure, a country doctor was almost anyone who called themselves that. Most learned by the apprentice system, and

---

*Snider graduated from Lakeview High School in 1898. While in his early twenties, he was elected Lakeview city recorder, then Lake County sheriff, and later a popular multiterm Oregon legislator. After serving in the legislature, he returned to his Paisley ranch and was actively involved in statewide grazing and land use issues. After his death in 1965, his ownership share of the ranch passed to his sister-in-law, Anna Jones. When she died a decade later, her will established the Anna F. Jones Educational Fund, modeled after the Daly Fund, intended to assure that students from Paisley would have support for college.

some were self-taught. Not only did Daly go to medical school, but he also was among the first to be licensed as a doctor, first in California just before arriving in Lakeview and then in Oregon in 1889.

As a doctor, Daly is probably best remembered for his heroism in responding to one of the worst catastrophes in Oregon history. On Christmas Eve in 1894, almost everyone who lived in or near Silver Lake gathered for a Christmas celebration at the community hall on the second floor of the town's general store. The hall's only entrance (and exit) was up a narrow outside staircase. It was a special gathering for a holiday dinner: a program of skits, music, and singing; a gift exchange; and a dance. It was well attended, with between 160 and 200 people who had come from as far as seventy miles away. Holiday decorations transformed the hall. Pine garlands hung on the walls, and a large Christmas tree was decorated with snowy cotton, paper chains, strings of popcorn, and hanging presents. In the soft glow of the oil-burning lamps, people sat on long wooden benches pushed close together.

At about eight o'clock in the evening, when the last Christmas carol had been sung and the three wise men were about to perform, George Payne, from neighboring Summer Lake, stood up on the bench to see his way to the door. As he rose, his head hit a large hanging oil lamp and sent it swinging. Burning oil rained down, igniting his clothes and splashing onto the pine floor. In a matter of seconds, it was a raging inferno, leading to a chaotic stampede for the one door to the stairs below. Those who made it to the door were crushed against it by the force of those behind them. At the same time, people outside were trying to force their way in to help. The door, which only opened inward, was stuck closed. Within six minutes, the stairway collapsed and the building was completely on fire. The only way out was to jump through a window. In less than an hour, the building was just smoking ruins. Forty people were dead and another thirty to forty were seriously injured. The town's only doctor, W. M. Thompson, was making a house call fifty miles away, and the supply of pain remedies and treatments that had been kept in the store had burned up in the fire.

Plans were quickly made to find medical care. One man rode to get Dr. Thompson. Another, Ed O'Farrell, a twenty-two-year-old cowboy, left on his horse to get Dr. Daly, who was a hundred miles away in Lakeview. It took nineteen hours for O'Farrell to ride at full gallop across the snowy desert in minus-twenty-degree weather, stopping only to change horses and make arrangements for fresh horses to be ready for Daly's return ride. He reached Lakeview at about four o'clock in the afternoon on Christmas Day. Shortly after O'Farrell's arrival, Daly left for Silver Lake. He went as far as Paisley by buckboard wagon and then on horseback the rest of the way. At times, the snow was as high as the horse's belly. He reached Silver Lake at six A.M. the next day and immediately began working with Dr. Thompson to treat the injured, who were being cared for in private homes and on pallets on the floor of the local saloon. It is said that all of the homes in the area had few or no linens left for the rest of the winter until the mule trains arrived in the spring with supplies, as their linens were used for bandages. Thanks to the heroic efforts of Dr. Daly and Dr. Thompson, many were saved.[8]

Neither Daly nor Thompson submitted any bills for their treatment of the injured. While he may not have been paid for his travels and work at the Silver Lake Fire, Daly did have a successful medical practice and a growing number of entrepreneurial activities; he was becoming known throughout the state for his political service and financial acumen.

In 1896, Daly was elected to the Oregon Senate, representing Lake, Crook, and Klamath Counties. Daly bested the well-known Republican, Oliver Cromwell Applegate, a member of the Applegate family credited with establishing the trail used by many settlers to reach the Oregon Territory. In the thirty-member Senate, Daly was one of only three Democrats, but he seemed to get along well with the Republicans. His long-time friend, Frank Light, used to tease Daly about his friendships with Republicans. Light remembered asking Daly why his best friends in Salem were Republicans. Daly replied, "The Republicans are in the majority and that is the way I get things done."[9]

Daly's first Senate session was a strange confluence of events. The Panic of 1893 led to a run on the banks and a severe credit crunch. President Grover Cleveland, a Democrat, was blamed for the resulting economic depression, which led to a Republican landslide in 1894 and the election of William McKinley, who, like other Republicans at the time, strongly supported the gold standard. The weakened Democratic Party gave rise to the Silverite movement, which advocated that silver should, along with gold, be the monetary standard. The Populist Party also supported a bimetallic monetary standard, and it was particularly strong in the West, where there were many farmers in debt and also many silver mines.* All of this resulted in an alliance of sorts between Democrats, Populists, and a few Republicans. Members of the Oregon alliance strategically absented themselves so there was never a quorum, which was needed for the Oregon House of Representatives to organize itself. The underlying reason for the alliance was a common interest in holding up the appointment of John Mitchell to the US Senate.** At the time, US senators were appointed to the Senate by each state legislature; direct election of US senators wouldn't come about until the Seventeenth Amendment in 1913. Since Mitchell, a Republican, had already come out in favor of the gold standard, the unexpected alliance was prepared to hold up his appointment. That is the reason the 1897 Oregon legislative session is known as the hold-up session and is why Oregon only had one US senator for two years.

The Senate, with its strong Republican majority, was able to organize, but without the House in session, no bills could be passed. The Senate session began on January 11, 1897, and Daly, as was his normal practice, was an energetic member. As it was when he was a representative in the state House, it was in his nature to be in attendance and attentive. On February 12, 1897, Daly wrote to his friend, Vinton Hall:

> In all probability it will be about the 10 of March before I can return to
> Lakeview and perhaps later because if the House of Representatives

---

*The more extreme Greenback Party advocated abandoning the gold standard in favor of non-backed paper money that could be printed and issued as part of national monetary policy. The party dissolved at the end of the nineteenth century, but the notion of separating the dollar from the gold standard was eventually adopted.

**Even for a politician, John Mitchell was quite a scoundrel. He graduated from college in Pennsylvania in the 1850s, and while working as a school teacher he impregnated one of his fifteen-year-old students. They quickly married and had two children. By 1857, he left teaching and was working as an attorney in a law firm. Apparently dissatisfied with his life in Pennsylvania, he absconded with $4,000 from his law firm, left his family, and took his mistress to California. However, in 1860, he tired of California, abandoned his mistress, and left for Oregon with their daughter. In Oregon, he married a local woman (without divorcing his wife in Pennsylvania) and went on to a seemingly successful career as a three-term US senator. All did not end well for Mitchell; he was indicted and convicted of conspiring to obtain and sell lands intended for homesteaders. He was never sentenced as he died during the appeal.

should organize it is the intention to remain in Session one or two or some three weeks after the forty days expires. If the House should not organize the Senate will adjourn our work from today.

The Senate did not adjourn that day. They continued in the hope that the House would organize itself. When it was apparent that would not happen, the Senate finally did adjourn on February 24 without having passed a single piece of legislation.

Daly returned to Lakeview, where he was quite busy. In addition to his medical practice and pharmacy, he was elected to a two-year term as mayor of Lakeview and was an active investor, loaning money to others in the community. In Daly's letter to Vinton Hall, who worked at Daly's pharmacy, Daly asked for Hall's help in purchasing county and town warrants (early municipal bonds):

> In regard to county and town warrants. I believe that it would be well to continue to buy the—paying par for town warrants and not to exceed 95 for county warrants and since we can buy Klamath warrants for 90 which are really as good as ours [Lakeview], I don't see the wisdom of paying even 95 for our warrants.

Issued as towns were incorporated, municipal bonds were relatively new and used to finance schools and roads. No doubt Daly was one of the first people in Lake County to make such investments, and it is likely that others learned about such investments through him. Daly was quite familiar with municipal bonds through his legislative work. Perhaps the most common legislation during Daly's time as a legislator was the passage of bills incorporating Oregon cities. Once incorporated, in addition to the right to tax, regulate, and prohibit all sorts of things, the new cities were able to issue bonds in support of schools, roads, and other infrastructure needs.

In those years, Daly was also beginning to serve as a banker. In his book on the informal history of banking in Oregon, O. K. Burrell referred to Bernard Daly as an example of how informal banking began in Oregon communities before the establishment of formal banks.

> In most of these early banks, private bankers did not suddenly become bankers. It is quite probable that sometimes men became bankers without planning to do so. In Lakeview, for example, Bernard Daly was a pioneer doctor who early in his career found it convenient and

profitable to lend his surplus funds to businessmen and ranchers at high interest rates. At some point, friends and associates began to entrust their funds to his care, which is merely another way of saying that he began to accept deposits. It is doubtful that Dr. Daly could have determined precisely the date on which banking operations began. In 1898 he incorporated the Bank of Lakeview, but this corporate entity merely continued the banking enterprise of Dr. Daly. It is quite probable that at some time the banking business was operated in Dr. Daly's medical office.[10]

Banks in Oregon were not subject to regulation until the Oregon Regulation Act of 1907 required the segregation of bank assets and liabilities from other assets and liabilities of the bank owners. Daly was ahead of his time when, on September 1, 1898, he established the Bank of Lakeview. It was a good time to establish a bank. The country and Lake County in particular had climbed out of the recession and the economic prospects for the new century were promising. Demand for cattle, driven by the post–Gold Rush growth of San Francisco, led to the sale of about thirty-five thousand head of Lake County cattle and brought nearly a million dollars into the county. The sale of sheep and wool brought the total even higher.[11] As the new century approached, the future of Lake County looked quite promising.

In the same month the bank was established, Daly once again left on the stage for Salem to attend a much-needed special session of the Oregon Senate. No state laws had been passed because of the hold-up session of 1897. In spite of being a Democrat in a Republican-controlled Senate, Daly was quite influential. He was nominated for Senate president and, although not elected, he did receive the votes of all of the Democratic and Populist senators and a couple of the Republican senators. He was chair of the Medicine, Pharmacy, and Dentistry Committee and a member of the Claims and Revision of Laws committees. As in prior sessions, he was rarely absent and fully engaged in the business of the Senate. And when the session ended on October 15, 1898, the last order of business was a resolution Daly introduced that thanked the Republican president of the Senate for "the courteous consideration he has shown the members of this body and impartial manner in which he has conducted the business of the senate during the time he has officiated as its presiding officer."[12]

Daly returned to Salem in early January for the start of the 1899 regular Senate session. Once again, he was viewed as the leading Democrat in a Senate with an overwhelming Republican majority. In addition to his regular committee service, Daly chaired a special Senate committee that investigated the management and condition of the Oregon Soldier's Home. One of the more controversial bills in that session was a reapportionment bill that disadvantaged the region Daly represented. In describing the debate over the bill, a reporter for the *Oregonian* wrote:

> It can hardly be called a hard-fought battle, for at no time was the event in doubt; but it was a bitterly fought battle, occupying almost the whole morning session and calling out more talk than any other measure up to this time.... if the advocates of the bill had been entirely frank, they would have said that now was their chance; that they had the votes and that no matter what considerations might be presented, the agreement already made to put the bill through would be enforced when the roll should be called. Viewed as a mere forensic display the incident was not without interest and Daly of Lake, in a protest against what he manifestly felt to be an outrage upon his county was perhaps the most truly imposing figure of all.[13]

Although Daly's protest was in vain, it is further evidence of his deep commitment to Lake County. The session ended, as it did the year before, with Daly introducing a resolution thanking the Senate president for the fair and impartial manner in which he conducted the business of the Senate.

Thirteen years after arriving in Oregon, Daly was a person of prominence, a well-respected politician, successful businessman, and rancher. As the new century approached, the future of Lake County and its adopted favorite son was looking good.

FUSION CONGRESSIONAL NOMINEE IN FIRST DISTRICT

BERNARD DALY, OF LAKEVIEW.

Bernard Daly, 1900 Candidate for US Congress. (Courtesy of the University of Oregon Historic Newspaper Archives)

CHAPTER 3

LATER YEARS IN LAKEVIEW
1900–1920

*A run for the US Congress. Taking a stand against the gold
standard. A terrible fire destroys most of Lakeview. Becoming
a judge and then a lawyer. Protecting the county from a
pandemic. Sheepshooters' War and a murder mystery.
Unblushing land fraud. The Narrow, Crooked, and Ornery.
Daly's relationship with Pearl Hall, the love of his life.*

As the nineteenth century drew to a close, Daly was well positioned for even greater political success. After serving in the Oregon House and Senate, he was a leader of the Democratic Party and respected by many of the state's Republicans. It was not at all surprising when he was selected to be the Democratic candidate for Congress in mid-April of 1900. Daly was often referred to as the "Fusion" candidate, reflecting the alliance between Democrats and Populists, most of whom opposed the gold standard and favored the coinage of silver. The gold standard was the wedge issue of the time; when Daly was nominated, it was unclear whether he favored the gold standard or a bimetallic standard that included silver. Just four years earlier when Daly was elected state senator in 1896, the *Oregonian* reported that Daly was among the "demo-populists" and was a sound-money Democrat, meaning he favored the gold standard.[1]

Identifying Daly as favoring the gold standard may have been wishful thinking by the *Oregonian*, a Republican-leaning paper. Describing Daly's May 13 campaign stop in Corvallis, the *Oregonian* reported that he declared himself in support of the Democratic platform and the free coinage of silver. The article went on to report that when Daly was asked if he intended to "take the stump," he responded, "It would be taking unfair advantage for me to go on the stump when Mr. Tongue [the incumbent] is at Washington attending to the state's business. If he were in Oregon, I should take the stump."[2]

Though Daly did not actively campaign, he did stop to visit with Democratic leaders in the Willamette Valley on his way back to Lakeview. When he reached

Medford, Daly received a telegram from his friend and business partner Vinton
Hall with the news that a terrible fire had devastated Lakeview on May 22.
Almost every business and house in town suffered damage from the fire with a
total of sixty-four buildings completely destroyed. Daly immediately made plans
to abandon his low-profile campaign and return to Lakeview to help rebuild. In
his letter to the State Democratic Committee, Daly wrote:

> The town of Lakeview, my home, has been almost totally destroyed
> by fire including the greater part of my property. I am, therefore, very
> sorry to inform you that I will be compelled, temporarily, at least, to
> retire from my canvass and return home.
>
> While I fully realize that my political interests may be materially
> affected thereby, I feel that a higher duty calls me to render such assis-
> tance as I am able to my friends and neighbors at home, many of whom
> have been left homeless by this great calamity.[3]

Daly returned to find Lakeview in ashes with almost the entire business portion of the town destroyed. While many of Daly's properties were destroyed, his
drugstore, which he operated with Vinton Hall, was one of the two businesses
that were saved—everything else had to be rebuilt.

As the former mayor and the founder and president of Lakeview Bank—and the
wealthiest man in the town—Daly provided much of the financing and leadership
for the rebuilding effort. Given his prominence and wealth, it is not surprising
that in addition to supporters, he also had enemies. An *Oregonian* article on the
politics of Lake County, published just before the fire, described the county's
position on Daly's run for Congress:

> The main fight this year is between Daly and Tongue. While it is
> Daly's home, he has many enemies here. They are making a desperate
> effort to carry the county against him. A stranger arriving here even
> before the campaign was thought of would never have expected to
> learn that Dr. Daly held office or would stand any show in this county.
> He is the most universally "cussed" man in the county. He is rarely
> ever spoken of favorably by any man. Yet he has been in office for more
> than 10 years and has never been defeated in this county for anything.
> There are no serious charges made against him, but everybody talks
> about Daly, and his enemies hate him worse than they do a snake.
> His friends say it is all jealousy. They say that Daly has accumulated

property here, always manages to succeed in whatever he undertakes, and that this has caused a jealousy that has grown to madness among his opponents. They declare they will defeat him this time, but a Daly man started out yesterday and offered to bet $50 with every man that would take him up that Daly would carry the county. The bet is public and notorious, but no man has yet covered it.[4]

As predicted, Daly did carry Lake County, but not the state, losing to Tongue by about three thousand votes in the June election. His heart really was not in it— he was deeply involved in the rebuilding of Lakeview and had just met Pearl Hall.

Bernard Daly in 1903, shortly after his election as county judge. (Courtesy of the Oregon Historical Society)

Bernard met Pearl through her brother, Vinton. Originally from Ohio, Pearl was a teacher and assistant principal in Medford. Bernard and Pearl had much in common. They both graduated from an Ohio college, Bernard from Ohio Normal in 1886 and Pearl from Wittenberg in 1888; the two colleges were somewhat similar and only sixty miles apart. Bernard was quite taken with Pearl, and from that point on, the two were constant companions. When they were not together in Lakeview because of Pearl's summer visits with her family or Bernard's business trips, they wrote to each other. It is through those letters, preserved at the University of Oregon Archives, that we learn about their loving relationship. The first was a letter from Bernard to Pearl on June 17, 1900, less than a month after the fire. That first letter and the others give a sense of his voice and manner, and the depth of his feelings for Pearl. It is a well-crafted handwritten five-page letter, a combination of news from Lakeview and his heart-felt feelings for her.

The letter begins and ends with his hopes for their relationship. "Today is Sunday and of course I wish above all things else the privilege of seeing you." The closing, "with kisses, I am, as before, your B." Tucked in between news of Pearl's brother and rebuilding of the town, Bernard expressed yet another hope—one that would not be realized. He was rooming with the Russel family, who were planning a move to nearby Alturas, California. Realizing he would need a new place to live, he made a suggestion. "If you were here I would request to board with you. Another boarder would help to pay expenses and what would be better still, I could dine with you and see you more often than otherwise."[5]

Unfortunately, we do not know how Pearl responded. The preserved correspondence is almost entirely one-sided. Of the forty-eight letters, only four were from Pearl to Bernard, all from the time in 1909 when Pearl traveled to Mexico. Pearl did write to him, but only his letters are preserved. Shortly after that first letter, Pearl did move to Lakeview but, to Bernard's disappointment, she did not board with him and instead lived with her brother, Vinton.

When Pearl began teaching in Lakeview in 1900, Oregon, was one of thirty-four states that had compulsory schooling laws, requiring children to attend through the completion of elementary school. There was no enforcement of the law, so many students were not enrolled; among those who were, only some attended regularly. About the time that Pearl started teaching in Lakeview, 145 students were enrolled, almost all in the primary grades. But the schools of

Lake County and all of Oregon were growing as the common school movement—the first major educational transformation—took hold. As chair of the school board, Daly was very involved in all aspects of the schools: financing, the hiring of teachers, and even the maintenance of school buildings. Long-time Lakeview teacher Alice Applegate Peil wrote about the first time she met Dr. Daly in 1902:

> I taught [in] a little three-month school six miles from Klamath Falls. The closing day of that school I received a telegram from the famous Dr. Daly asking me to come to Lakeview. Their teacher was unable to handle her pupils and had been asked to resign. I accepted.
>
> At 7 A.M., December 7, 1902, I boarded the stage, a two-horse hack with just a top and no curtains. The snow was coming down like a blanket. We started on the 110-mile trip through mud and snow. The roads were not even graveled. I traveled all day, reaching Bly at midnight. There I took the next vehicle to leave, a two-horse, two-seated buckboard with no cover. The driver was a little Dutchman who never uttered a word and sat alone on the front seat. Going over Devil's Garden was so rough that I could not keep a blanket over my knees. Reaching Lakeview at 3 P.M. I felt so numb that I could scarcely walk, let alone change my clothes.
>
> But I had to dress to make my first appearance before the great Dr. Daly as I had to teach the next day. To the young teacher of that era he was a most important personage.
>
> Here I found the same big square four-room type of schoolhouse and same equipment as before [in Klamath] except that the transom glass was broken out. I asked Dr. Daly, who was chairman of the school board, to replace the glass. He said in the most dignified manner, "Miss Applegate, can't you stuff some paper into it?"[6]

Being frugal and busy were essential to Daly's character. Though he was still working—as a doctor, president of the Bank of Lakeview, and manager of properties, including his ranch to the east of Lakeview—and was chair of the school board, he ran for the position of county judge and won by a considerable margin. As county judge in remote Lake County, Daly was essentially the chief executive of the county, very much like a governor for an area that was larger than several states. It was a time when counties were quite independent. Oregon's state government was still relatively new and weak. Roads and communications were poor, and Lake County was far from Salem.

Once elected, Daly set to work with his usual sense of strategic vision, attention to detail, and frugality. Daly's frugalness was legendary. He lived in a small room, ate the cheapest meals on the menus of the local restaurants, and spent very little money on himself. His frugal ways were a great help when he inherited a county budget that was deeply in debt. In a letter to the editor of a local paper describing his candidacy, Daly wrote:

> I believe it should be the earnest and determined duty of the county court to reduce the expenses of the county with a view to the gradual extinction of our present indebtedness, without increasing taxation, so that when free from debt the taxpayer may enjoy a substantial reduction in his taxes; that the county court should, in a business way, devote itself diligently to a careful and thorough investigation of the various branches under its jurisdiction.[7]

As promised, Daly led the county out of debt in just three years without raising taxes. While he seemed to have the Midas touch, it was actually his attention to detail and frugalness. The court journals reveal how he cut costs and raised revenue without raising taxes. County offices that had been ordering supplies by express shipping were required to use standard shipping and to provide the court with records and weights of all shipped items. Unfunded state mandates, including paying for coyote scalps, were no longer paid; required licensing fees and taxes were diligently collected, including taxes on a great many transient sheep that grazed in the county.

Daly seemed to be involved in everything of consequence. In early May of 1903, Daly wrote the state health officer to notify him of a case of smallpox in Silver Lake; he reported that the patient and all exposed persons were quarantined. Convinced that the case came from Crook County, where there were many cases and little or no effort to quarantine those who had been exposed, Daly strongly urged the state health officer to travel to Crook County and establish strict quarantines for all exposures. If not, Daly said he would issue a quarantine to prevent all ingress from that infected area.

The next day, Daly received a telegram saying to go ahead and establish the quarantine if he thought it was best. He did. On May 6, he ordered George Hanan to "proceed to the north line of Lake County, near the McCarty place,

on the stage road, and to establish and maintain at such place a quarantine station, and to prevent ingress of any and all persons, including stages carrying the
United States mails and all other things from said Crook county."[8]

It is not clear how long the quarantine remained in place or how effective
it was, but it was quite progressive for its time. With Daly's urging, the Lake
County Board of Health required isolation and quarantine for all exposed to
smallpox and strongly recommended that all residents be vaccinated. It was a
time when many believed that smallpox was associated with poverty and filth;
some thought it was caused by planetary misalignment. Though vaccination with
cowpox was found to be effective, many resisted. Daly was a doctor long before
he became a judge. As a doctor, he knew, understood, and believed in germ theory and knew that disease could be spread from person to person by microorgan-
isms that couldn't be seen.

In addition to being a doctor, banker, and judge, Daly was also a rancher, or
at least the owner of a ranch. While it is unlikely he ever roped a cow or branded
a steer, Daly did organize and serve as president of the Lake County Land
and Livestock Company which owned the twelve-thousand-acre 7T Ranch in
Warner Valley. As is true of many other Lake County ranches, the 7T had both
sheep and cattle, but with increasing demand for beef in California, the sale of
cattle was becoming more profitable. With what may have been a bit of bragging,
Daly reported on his beef sales in an October 1904 letter to Pearl Hall:

> Mr. Miller [7T Ranch foreman] has returned from delivering our cat-
> tle, and another beef buyer has gone over to the ranch to purchase the
> rest of our cattle. We expect to sell about $10,000 worth this time
> which will complete our beef sales for the year.[9]

Having both sheep and cattle on his ranch while serving as the county judge
must have given Daly perspective on the range war that peaked in the early
1900s. It really was a war, though mostly one-sided as almost all the casualties
were sheep.

In the late 1800s, groups of cattlemen in Eastern Oregon formed vigilante
groups called Sheepshooters with the goal of eliminating the sheep and anyone
who tried to stop them. Between 1895 and 1906, the Sheepshooters killed at
least twenty-five thousand sheep. The violence reached a climax in 1904 when
masked men killed about two thousand sheep on a cold February night near
Silver Lake in northern Lake County. A month later, Creed Conn, a prominent

Silver Lake merchant, disappeared; some seven weeks after his disappearance, he was found dead from gunshot wounds. Many blamed his death on the
Sheepshooters. There had been reports that Conn had knowledge of the sheep
killers and was about to tell his brother, Lafayette Conn, the district attorney.
It was a big story—Creed Conn's prominence and the strange circumstances of
his disappearance and death made for sensational news with articles appearing
on the front page of the *Oregonian* for nine months. As county judge, Daly was
certainly involved in the case. Vinton Hall was one of the doctors who examined
the body, and a coroner's jury ruled that it was suicide. But many continued to
believe it was murder, and that the Sheepshooters were involved.

More than a hundred years later, Melany Tupper, Lake County author and
amateur sleuth, spent years investigating the case, digging through old newspaper articles and court records. In her book, *The Sandy Knoll Murder: Legacy
of the Sheepshooters*, she makes a compelling argument that Conn did not com-
mit suicide and was not killed by the Sheepshooters, but instead murdered by
Ray Jackson, a Silver Lake school teacher.* Unknown to people in Silver Lake,
Jackson was a convicted thief and embezzler who had served two terms in the
Oregon State Penitentiary. Given his criminal record, it is likely that he went to
remote Lake County to get a fresh start. His career as a teacher in Silver Lake was
cut short when, in 1908, he was elected Lake County School Superintendent, a
position he held until 1911, when he was indicted for embezzling money from
the school district. Melany Tupper's investigations show how Jackson was personally involved with six suspicious homicides—three of which were declared
suicides (including Conn's) and three of which remain officially unsolved.[10]
We'll never know for sure, but it does seem that the Sheepshooters lived up to
their name—they killed sheep, not people.

Ray Jackson was able to escape his checkered past because Lake County was
far from the beaten path. At the beginning of the twentieth century, Lakeview

---

*Jackson had breakfast with Conn on the morning of his murder and was the last person
to have spoken with him. Many of the circumstances of Conn's death were suspicious.
Though it was ruled a suicide, it would seem difficult for a person to shoot himself twice
with a single-action revolver and then beat one's own face to a bloody pulp. And Conn,
at the time of his death, was trying to figure out what happened to the proceeds of a
$3,000 loan missing from his bank account. The money was never found, but Jackson
bought about $3,000 worth of cattle shortly after Conn's disappearance. At the time,
many thought the coroner's jury ruling of suicide was in concern for protecting cattle
interests.

had the dubious distinction of being the county seat in the United States that was farthest from a railroad. In 1906, there were three ways to get to Lakeview and each involved long and difficult stage rides. It was a time when railroads were being built throughout the country and there was over-the-top enthusiasm in Lakeview every time survey crews and railroad representatives visited the county. Speculation was especially widespread from 1905 to 1910, with articles regularly appearing in the local paper, each projecting population growth and prosperity that would be sure to come with the railroad.

In was during those times, in February of 1909, that Pearl Hall left Lakeview and went to Mexico City, where she hoped to teach and study Spanish. From the first of four letters to Daly, it seems that her initial plans were open-ended as she wrote, "I do not know when I shall return to the U.S. Very likely when my money gets short I will start. If I can get a position I shall remain some time."[11] In the letter she wrote of the challenges of learning Spanish. Pearl had hoped to learn from her landlady, a French woman who moved to Mexico some time before. According to Pearl, her landlady had picked up Spanish from "domestics," but since Pearl wanted to learn a purer Spanish, she took lessons at the Berlitz School. In her next letter, just a few weeks later, she reported that she studied Spanish about four hours a day and had arranged to exchange English lessons for Spanish lessons. She was also searching for a job and wrote to Daly, telling him that she turned down a job as a governess; she also asked him to write her a recommendation that described her teaching at the primary and more advanced grades.

In her third letter, written in early March, Pearl again reported on her language studies but acknowledged that Spanish was not a language that "can be learned in six weeks." There is quite a gap between this letter and the fourth and final one dated August 13, 1909; perhaps there were other letters that were not preserved. Pearl began the fourth letter with a paragraph in Spanish about her language studies and her plans to return to Oregon the next week. Pearl did return to Lakeview in the fall of 1909, just as the county was about to receive a huge economic boost.

Pearl returned to Lakeview at an extraordinary time. That fall, Lakeview was the site of the largest private land auction sale ever held in the United States, or possibly anywhere in the world. Referred to as "unblushing land fraud" in an 1888 *New York Times* article, it was a case of fraud on top of fraud. After the forced removal of Native Americans from their lands, the federal government promoted settlements in the West through land grants to individuals for homesteads and to states for colleges and, in the case of Oregon, military roads. Between 1865 and 1869, Congress awarded land grants to Oregon to pass on to companies that constructed military wagon roads for use by troops during emergencies. Under the terms of the grant, as soon as a company completed a ten-mile stretch of road, it could apply to the governor for certification. If the road were deemed suitable for wagon use, the company received three sections, about two thousand acres, of land for every mile of road as payment. What actually happened was more guided by speculation and fraud than by getting from point to point. Surveyors laid out indirect routes designed to pass through as much well-watered, desirable land as possible. The Oregon Central Military Road meandered through Goose Lake Valley and over the Warner Mountains in Lake County. Though the road was certified by Oregon's governor in 1870, it was little more than a rudimentary trail. In reality, the Oregon Central Military Road was a giant scam, designed to acquire public lands at little or no cost.

It was a national scandal that led to a congressional investigation and ultimately a Supreme Court case that resulted in the US government reclaiming lands that were not yet titled. Much of that titled land was acquired by the Oregon Valley Land Company and then subdivided into fourteen thousand parcels totaling 340,000 acres that were sold at a week-long auction in September of 1909 in Lakeview. Some fifteen hundred people came from throughout the country to attend the auction in person; hundreds more submitted bids from afar. When it was over, about fifteen thousand parcels were sold, many of which included a lot in the town of Lakeview. The sale of town lots greatly added to the tax revenue, at least for the first year or so. In spite of promises of large-scale irrigation that would transform dry lands into what was described as "the future garden spot of the Northwest,"[13] much of the land was worthless. Very few of the purchasers ever lived on the property or used it for farming or ranching.

The economic boom did help Daly in his efforts to build a new and grand county courthouse. It was a beautiful three-story red brick courthouse with a clock tower.[14] Daly was rightly proud of the new courthouse, especially since it was built without assuming any debt. He sent a specially made post card with a photo of the courthouse to Pearl in Mexico: "Doesn't this look natural. It is even more nearly completed now. Has the clock and chimes, a new iron fence, and they are cleaning off the yard."[15]

The new courthouse with its clock tower projected a grandness that reflected the hopes for future growth and prosperity. Finally, after a decade of waiting, the Nevada, California, and Oregon Railroad (NCO) announced in December 1909 that it would extend its route an additional sixty miles from Alturas, California, to Lakeview. The NCO began in 1880 with investors and a plan to build a railroad line from Reno to the northern border of Oregon on the Columbia River. It was a time of great expansion and speculation in railroads. The railroad industry was the nation's largest employer outside of the agricultural sector, and speculative investments in railroads both fueled the economy and contributed to the financial panic of 1893.*

The NCO suffered from mismanagement and corruption. In what could be described as a hostile takeover, a fight broke out at a contentious board meeting. Two people were shot, one of whom, the company secretary, died. According to reports, the bodies were removed, and the meeting went on to elect a new board. Always short of cash, construction was slow. It took about twenty-five years for the NCO to reach Alturas, just south of the Oregon border, and another five to reach Lakeview in January 1912. Lakeview celebrated with Railroad Day on January 7, when 225 people came on an excursion train from Reno. Many in the crowd wore badges that read, "Welcome N-C-O to Lakeview, the City of Destiny: You have seen our snows; Come again to see our flowers."[16]

Rail access south to California through Reno did contribute to the growth of Lake County cattle, sheep, and lumber industries, but the NCO never expanded farther north than Lakeview. Continuing financial troubles and the use of narrow-gauge tracks rather than standard-width tracks all contributed to the demise of the NCO, which had become commonly known as the "narrow, crooked, and ornery." In 1925, it was sold to the Southern Pacific Company, the tracks were converted to standard gauge, and it continued operation until 1985.

Through it all, Daly remained busy. There was his work as county judge, president of the bank, owner of a ranch, and school board member. As if that were not enough, while in his early fifties, he began studying for the bar exam, which

---

*The financial panic of 1893 is considered the end of the Gilded Age. By mid-1894, one-quarter of all US railroads had failed. Acquisition of the bankrupt companies led to the consolidation of the industry. In 1906, two-thirds of all rail mileage in the United States was controlled by seven entities, with J.P. Morgan holding the largest portion.

Bernard Daly in 1915 when, after serving as Lake County judge for thirteen years, he was appointed to serve as the first circuit court judge for the newly formed Lake County Circuit Court. (Courtesy of OSU Libraries Special Collections & Archives Research Center)

he took and passed in 1911. He was also involved in major community events. At a Lakeview suffragette meeting in 1912, Daly spoke in favor of granting women the right to vote. This excerpt is from his handwritten notes for the talk, which Pearl Hall saved and are now in the University of Oregon Archives:

> I hope that Oregon will follow the example of the great states of California on the south and Washington on north by granting to them [women] all of the rights and privileges of citizenship.
>
> All history points to the fact that woman is intellectually man's equal and morally his superior, and that her abilities have enabled her to occupy any position from the lowest to the loftier.

The election of 1912 was the sixth time that women's right to vote was on the ballot; it finally passed by a slim majority, making Oregon one of fifteen states that granted women the right to vote before the passage of the Nineteenth Amendment in 1920.

Throughout his life, Daly was very conservative with financial matters but quite liberal when it came to social issues. In 1896, he responded to a lengthy alumni survey from his alma mater, Ohio Normal University. One of the questions asked about his politics and religious inclinations. He responded, "Democrat, liberal thinker, belong to no church."

Daly served as county judge for thirteen years, from 1902 until 1915, when Governor Withycombe, a Republican, appointed him to serve as the first circuit court judge for the newly formed Lake County Circuit Court. Anticipating criticism for appointing Daly, a Democrat, Withycombe said he was of the opinion that the judiciary should be nonpartisan.

In 1916, Daly ran for reelection as circuit court judge but lost to Lafayette Conn, the district attorney. After having served in elected offices since shortly after his arrival in Lakeview, Daly lost an election in Lake County for the first time—the last time he would run for public office. But it was not the end of his public service. He continued serving on the school board, a position he held for a remarkable nine consecutive terms, totaling thirty years, up to 1919, just shortly before he died. Daly also chaired the Lake County Liberty Bond campaign that raised money for the war effort. It was part of a massive national effort that raised about $24 billion, the equivalent of more than $5 trillion today. The Liberty Bond campaign depended on local leadership and contributions from a broad range of American households. To make the bonds more accessible, a fifty-dollar Liberty Bond could be purchased through a subscription with an initial payment of four dollars, then twenty-three weekly payments of two dollars.*

With Daly chairing the drive and also being one of the state's largest purchasers of bonds, Lake County led the entire state in meeting and exceeding subscriptions. County targets for subscriptions were established by state liberty loan committees, typically based on total county banking capital. With participation from about 30 percent of Lake County's population (probably representing more than half of all households),** Lake County far exceeded its quota.[17] In April of 1918, the *Oregonian* reported:

> Lake County is going strong in rolling up liberty loan totals. Bernard Daly, county chairman for the third drive, telegraphed headquarters yesterday that the quota assigned that county has been so far oversubscribed that now the county stands at 400 percent of its allotted total. "Subscriptions are still coming in fast," said Mr. Daly. "The total amounts to $75 for every man, woman, and child in the county."[18]

Daly's reputation for financial savviness was such that he was often called upon by friends in San Francisco for financial advice. In March 1919, Daly traveled to San Francisco for business. As was his custom whenever he traveled, he wrote to Pearl.*** In his March 19 letter, he mentioned his lunch at the new Fairmont Hotel. On a future visit, he hoped Pearl would join him for dinner at the Fairmont, though, as he said in the letter, "probably the dinner may cost me my pile but shall spend it so you may have one meal in the most beautiful hotel I have ever seen." Somewhat less than a year later, the two would go to San Francisco together, but, sadly, they never did have that dinner at the Fairmont. Daly's "pile" would be used for something else.

---

*Adjusting for inflation, $50 in 1919 is equivalent to around $700 today, about the price of a major household appliance.

**Economist Eric Hilt reports that Lake County's participation rate of 29.1 percent of population far exceeded the average of 16.8 percent for all US counties in his analysis.

***During one particularly long visit to San Francisco in 1912, he wrote a lengthy letter each day.

CHAPTER 4

FROM THE ROARING TWENTIES INTO A DEEP DEPRESSION 1920s–1930s

Daly's death. The will. The challenge. A promise fulfilled.
The blacksmith's son becomes one of America's leading
patent attorneys. A college-going culture forms.
The Depression depletes the scholarship funds.
A kid from Lakeview guides objects in space.

In early January of 1920, after having been ill since just before Christmas, Daly "went below," taking the train to San Francisco to be treated by specialists. He was accompanied by Dr. Charles Liethead, his Lakeview physician; Fred Reynolds, his longtime business partner; and Pearl Hall, the love of his life. Daly never made it to San Francisco. He died en route, near Livermore, California, at 5:30 A.M. on Monday, January 5. On the following Sunday, a crowd of about seven hundred—almost everyone who lived in or near Lakeview—attended his memorial service.*

Over the years, there had been much speculation about what Daly would do with his wealth. In a 1939 interview, his longtime friend Frank Light remembered discussing estate planning with Daly. In commenting about a relatively small estate that had caused quarrels among the heirs, Light said to Daly, "since it was a small estate, let them scrap but large property owners should make a careful and proper disposal of their property before their death. Now you for instance, all your money will go to your relatives in Chicago, to a country which you said you hated after your last trip east. Someone else will enjoy your money." Daly replied, "Don't you think so. When I pass away it won't go back to Chicago."[1]

Although it was common knowledge that Daly was wealthy, the amount of his wealth was the subject of much speculation and some controversy. The contrast

---

* The population of Lakeview in 1920 was 1,139.

between Daly's frugal ways and his position of prominence drew attention to his wealth and also caused some jealousy and ill will. During campaigns for the position of county judge, it was common for his opponents to claim that, in spite of his wealth, Daly only paid a minimal amount of taxes. In 1910, the *Lakeview Herald* printed this report on Daly's taxes:

> It seems that certain parties have already begun the usual campaign reports about Dr. Daly, saying that he only pays $100 of taxes. As a matter of fact Sheriff Dent certifies that he has paid during this year, on last year's assessment, directly and other interests which he owns, the sum of $1,752.66 which sum is the largest amount paid by any individual residing in Lake County. When it is remembered that the tax rate is 7.9 mills, it will show that his assessment, at that rate, would be $221,855.69.[2]

While the amount of Daly's wealth was a mystery, there was no doubt that he was wealthy. Since he had never married and had no direct heirs, people wondered where the money would go. A couple of days after Christmas, on December 27, 1919, just ten days before his death, Daly signed his will and it was, as Light had suggested, carefully crafted. In five typewritten pages, the will contained ten bequests and six instructions. The first of the bequests were as might be expected: $1,000 each to his brother, Hugh, and to five nephews and nieces; $5,000 to Pearl Hall and a continuing $2,000 each year for the remainder of her life. Next was a bequest of $1,200 each year to the Lakeview Public Hospital for ten years, and a bequest to the Bank of Lakeview of the land on which it was located.

Following these bequests were the instructions that his stock in the Bank of Lakeview be kept intact as far as possible and that his executors, W. P. Heryford, J. D. Heryford, and Fred Reynolds (all members of the Bank of Lakeview board), vote Daly's share of the bank stock. Always the careful manager, Daly further specified that, should there be a disagreement among the executors, those holding the larger share of stock should decide the question.

Next was the heart of the will. All of Daly's property was to be sold and converted into cash, invested in municipal bonds, and combined with Daly's other investments and placed in a fund to be known as the Bernard Daly Educational Fund, the annual income from which would be used for college scholarships for Lake County youth:

It is my desire and I now direct and will that any and all income from said Bernard Daly Fund, except only such amounts as may be necessary to satisfy the bequests set forth in this will and the expenses of administration, be used, payed [sic.] out and applied by the trustees hereinafter named, from year to year as such income accrues, in educating worthy young men and women of Lake County, Oregon, in the schools, colleges, and technical schools of the state of Oregon, bearing all their expenses through school, if necessary, until their education is completed; such students to be recommended by the County Judge and County School Superintendent of Lake County, Oregon, their recommendation, however, not to be binding on my trustees. It is my desire that as many students, as possible, not less than fifteen each and every year, take advantage of this provision of this will, with this proviso, however, that such trustees always maintain a sufficient reserve so that it will not be necessary for any scholar to quit school before his or her education is completed for lack of funds.[3]

The vision that not less than fifteen students would have all of their expenses provided for all four years of college was extraordinary. There was no scholarship like that anywhere in Oregon or perhaps in the entire country. To get a sense of just how extraordinary it was, the 1922–1923 University of Oregon catalog identified only two scholarship funds available to students. One was the new Daly Fund that would provide full funding each year for four years to at least fifteen students from Lake County. The other was the Mary Spiller Scholarship, which covered room and board for one student for one year. The predominant type of student aid at the University of Oregon and all other colleges at the time was interest-free loans. In that same year, twelve loan funds were available at the University of Oregon, none of which provided full funding for all four years.[4] The Daly Fund was unique.

The day after Daly's funeral, his will was filed for probate with the Lake County clerk. The next day, the *Lake County Examiner* printed Daly's will in its entirety, noting that the value of Daly's estate was about a million dollars. Soon most people in the county knew that Daly had amassed a much larger fortune than they had imagined, and instead of leaving the money to relatives, he was giving most of it to the youth of Lake County so they could go to college. Within days, families were asking how they could apply for the funds.

The awarding of scholarships would have to wait, however, as Daly's will was challenged by Daly's relatives, including his only remaining sibling, Hugh Daly, and fourteen nephews and nieces from many different states as well as from Ireland, Scotland, England, Canada, and Italy. The five nieces and nephews identified in the will would have been notified of their bequests of $1,000 each. Likely to have been motivated by the large size of the estate, they went to some lengths to contact all of Daly's living relatives and organize a challenge to the will.

At the time, the size of the estate was estimated to be close to a million dollars. How much would that be today? Economists have proposed different ways to calculate the value of money over time. Some are based on the rate of inflation, some on the cost of a set bundle of goods, and others on wages for labor. Depending on which formula is used, a million dollars in 1920 would today be equivalent to at least $12 million and perhaps as much as $250 million. That's quite a range of values, but there is no doubt that it was a lot of money at that time, and especially in Lakeview, Oregon.

Several months before the challenge to the will was filed, the first meeting of the Daly Fund trustees was held in Portland on September 11, 1920. As specified in Daly's will, the trustees were members of the Bank of Lakeview board of directors and the presidents of Oregon Agricultural College and the University of Oregon. As noted in the minutes of the meeting, the trustees discussed the awarding of scholarships but decided against doing so because of the likelihood that relatives would challenge the will and because of the opinion issued by the Oregon attorney general that the trust fund, although for charitable purposes, would be subject to an inheritance tax of approximately $180,000. At the meeting, the trustees approved a constitution; appointed standing committees for investments, finance, designation of schools, and selection of students; and elected officers: president Fred Reynolds, Daly's longtime business partner; vice-president W. J. Kerr, president of Oregon Agricultural College; and secretary-treasurer F. W. Payne, a Bank of Lakeview director.

Because the complainants included citizens of other states and foreign countries, it was assigned to the federal district court in Portland on December 23, 1920, where Judge Robert Bean presided. The challenge to the will was based on three major complaints: 1) That the beneficiaries of the trust (scholarship recipients) are uncertain because it is not clear how scholarship applicants will be deemed worthy; 2) the plan of the intended scholarship fund is so ill defined as to be incapable of execution; and 3) that a trust for private ends (Bank of Lakeview stock) is intermingled with a charitable trust thereby rendering both void.

Attorneys representing the defendants (the executors for Daly's will and Daly Fund trustees) filed a motion to dismiss the complaint on February 9, 1921. Two months later, on April 25, Judge Bean issued his opinion supporting the motion of the defendants to dismiss the complaint. In response to the complaint that the beneficiaries of the trust (the scholarship recipients) are uncertain because the testator (Daly) had not declared who shall be considered worthy, Judge Bean cited prior case law:

> A public charity begins only when uncertainty in the recipient begins, and while in a private trust the gift will fail and revert to the donor or to his heirs, when the beneficiaries are so uncertain, or so incapable of taking, that they cannot be identified or cannot legally claim its benefits, yet in the case of a charitable gift it is immaterial that the beneficiaries are indefinite.

Regarding the selection process, Judge Bean wrote:

> [Daly] designated the class which should be the recipients of his bounty, provided the method of selection for such class, leaving the details to be settled by his trustees. Thus we have a given trust with a trustee, a particular purpose—education—and a designated class as beneficiaries, and hence a good trust for charitable uses.

And, finally, Judge Bean did not find evidence of any improper intermingling of private and charitable funds.

On the very next day, April 26, the state's major newspaper, the *Oregonian*, reported that the challenge to the will had been dismissed and that somewhat more than $40,000 would be available each year for scholarships. In the article, the attorney for the defendants, Lair Thompson, was quoted as saying: "The county will always be sparsely settled and is remote from the higher educational institutions of the state. President Campbell of the University of Oregon, who is one of the trustees to administer the fund, recently expressed the view that Lake County is perhaps the only county in the United States with a fund sufficient to insure an opportunity for [higher] education to all the young men and women of the county."[5]

Following the judge's ruling, the relatives were to have six months, until November of 1921, to appeal. But, in November, the executors of the estate were told that a clerk in the federal court had failed to file Judge Bean's judgment so the contestants would have another six months, until May of 1922, during which they could appeal. The time passed without an appeal, and the trustees announced they would make the scholarship selections at their June meeting in Lakeview.

On June 29, all of the trustees attended the meeting, including the presidents of Oregon Agricultural College and the University of Oregon, each of whom made the three-day trip to Lakeview.* At the meeting, in accordance with the will, the trustees reviewed the recommendations of the county judge and county school superintendent, and awarded scholarships of $600 to nineteen of the thirty-eight applicants. There were only twenty-two Lake County high school graduates that year, but applications from graduates from the two prior years were also considered. The annual scholarship award of $600 was quite generous—enough to cover all expenses, including laundry and two trips home.

If you were to walk into the Lake County School District offices today, one of the first things you would see is a framed photo collage of the scholarship recipients in the 1920s and 1930s, including the 1922 recipients. A photo of Bernard Daly is in the center of the collage, and all around his photo are professionally taken photos of serious-looking young men and women dressed in their finest. Looking at the photo of the 1922 recipients, you'll notice that most were young women that year (and all through the 1920s and '30s). Nationally, only about two percent of the college-age cohort (eighteen to twenty-four) went to college in those days, and most were young men. So why did so many young women receive the Daly scholarship?

In the 1920s, less than 20 percent of America's youth graduated from high school; in Lake County, where many boys worked on family ranches, far fewer boys than girls went on to high school. Since the direct costs of attending college were low and the scholarship funds were plentiful, most of the 1922 high school graduates and some from previous years who wanted to go to college received

---

*Travel to and from Lakeview was time consuming and costly, requiring about three days of travel each way by rail and stage. After completing a trip to attend the 1923 Trustee meeting, OAC President Kerr filed a claim for reimbursement of $80.95 for his travel, lodging, and meals, which, in terms of both time and money, would have likely made it one of his most expensive trips of the year.

Photo collage of the 1922 Daly scholarship recipients. Cornelia "Connie" Robertson is the second from the bottom, on the left. (Courtesy of the Lake County School District)

scholarship—and most of those high school graduates were young women. Given the thinking of the time, if there had only been one or two scholarships available, it is likely they would have gone to the young men. The pattern of more young women than men continued until the 1940s. It's likely that during the 1920s and '30s, the most educated women in Oregon, and perhaps the entire Northwest, were in Lake County, Oregon.

Look a little closer at the photo collage, and you'll see Cornelia (Connie) Robertson on the lower left. Yes, the very same Connie Robertson who, one year before his death, talked with Dr. Daly at the telegraph office while he waited for the night rates to go into effect. When she told him that she would like to go

Connie Robertson high school yearbook
photo with the inscription, "Cornelia
Robertson, whom nothing can rile, For on
her face there is always a smile." (Courtesy
of the Lake County School District)

to college and study medicine but that her parents could never afford it, Daly told her not to worry; he promised that there would be a way. After graduating from high school in 1921, she taught elementary school for a year and then was among the first to receive the scholarship in 1922. Daly's promise was fulfilled.

Connie was one of seven students who went to the University of Oregon that year; six went to Oregon Agricultural College and six to Oregon State Normal School. Connie wrote home almost every week, and, thanks to her family who kept her letters, there is a record of her college experiences. Connie's letters, most of which were to her mother, were each several pages long and rich with descriptions of her classes, life in the residence hall, and her social and academic activities. Shortly after classes started, she wrote to her sister, Joycelin:

> I went to the Freshman dance last night and had a dandy time. Saw the whole Lake County representatives and had a dance with them. You would be surprised to see the way Tom Holder is stepping around here, he dances so much better than I thought he would. I met several other interesting Freshmen and we each came home with a Frosh man. I don't think I will tell you who I saw and what I did anymore because I'm afraid it will get in the paper. I nearly fell over last night when the kids told me that they were over at the Library yesterday and saw in the Examiner [Lake County Examiner] some of the junk that I wrote home.[6]

The experiences of the Lake County kids who went to college were big news back home, and it seems that some of the news from Connie's letters had made it into the local paper. That didn't stop the steady flow of letters from Connie to her family, although it may have influenced what she wrote. Connie, who was studying science with the expectation of going to medical school, also wrote to her mother about what she was learning:

> I learned something interesting in Chem. Lab this morning that I think will interest you also. We were studying mercury this morning and this is what I found out. Corrosive sublimate is composed of mercury and chlorine and so is calomel. But corrosive sublimate is a little different in that it has more chlorine in it and dissolves more easily. It was for a long time used as an antiseptic but it has been proven now that it also destroys the tissues so its extensive use has been discontinued. I have decided that I don't want any more calomel.[7]

Connie finished her degree at the University of Oregon in three years; then, after graduating from the University of Oregon Medical School in Portland in 1929, she interned at the Women's and Children's Hospital in San Francisco. In 1930, Connie moved to New York City, where she worked at a medical office on Park Avenue and also at the Presbyterian Columbia Medical Center.

Connie's younger sister, Joycelin, graduated from Lakeview High School in 1924 and, as her sister, received the Daly scholarship and attended the University of Oregon, where she planned to study prelaw. After struggles with the required quick speaking skills, Joycelin visited with her sister, who was in medical school, and then changed her major to medicine. After graduating from the University of Oregon, Joycelin also went to the medical school in Portland and then worked in New York at the Columbia Medical School while she and Connie lived together in an apartment in Greenwich Village. What a time to be in Greenwich Village, already known as the place to be for budding artists, speakeasies, and jazz clubs. It must have felt like a long way from Lakeview, Oregon.

It was quite remarkable for those two women from Lakeview to become doctors at a time when less than 5 percent of doctors were women. Working in New York, Connie and Joycelin were at the top of their profession. They both were among the first to receive national board certification, established in 1933—first in the specialties of dermatology, obstetrics, and gynecology. Very few doctors were board certified in those times; today about 85 percent are. Connie and Joycelin were definitely ahead of their time.

After working in New York for six years, Joycelin returned to Lakeview, where she opened a general practice and was active in obstetrics at the Robertson Maternity Home, operated by her mother, who no doubt had influenced the girls and their younger brother, Lewis, to become doctors. Connie moved to San Diego in 1942 and then in 1956, she too returned to Lakeview to help care for her mother. After getting her Oregon medical license, she practiced with her sister and younger brother.

Connie lived life to the fullest. In Lakeview, in addition to her medical practice, she was an active member of the Soroptimists investment club, the local historical society, and several card clubs. Among other things, she was known for her extensive hat collection and flashy pink Thunderbird. She died in 2001, shortly after celebrating her ninety-eighth birthday. According to her niece,

These photos of Dr. Cornelia "Connie" Robertson (left) and Dr. Joycelin "Jockey" Robertson (right) hang on the wall of the Lake District Hospital along with photos of all the doctors (including their brother, Lawrence) who have served the Lake County community. (Courtesy of the Lake District Hospital)

Janice (Decker) Kniskern (LHS 1963), she was fond of saying, "I was able to do what I wanted in my life which is more than some people can say."

Not all of the women who received the Daly scholarship became doctors, but, as with Connie and Joycelin, access to college did give them more choices in their lives at a time when women had just gained the right to vote after decades of struggle and state-by-state deliberations. Mabel Peterson graduated from Lakeview High School with Joycelin in 1924 and also went to the University of Oregon, where she majored in education. Mabel's daughter, Arlee, described her mother as "one of the original women's libbers." Mabel was a teacher, a librarian, a poet, and an activist in support of women's rights and the emancipatory power of education. She insisted that her younger siblings needed to go to college, and they did—all eight of the Peterson kids went to college.

It wasn't only the young women from Lake County who did well—so did the young men. One of the fifteen 1923 scholarship recipients was Virgil Woodcock, son of the Lakeview blacksmith, Eldon Woodcock. As was true of so

many others in those days, it was unlikely that Virgil would have gone to college
without the Daly scholarship. In the fall of 1923, Virgil left Lakeview for Oregon
Agricultural College, where he majored in electrical engineering. After graduating in 1927, he worked for General Electric in the Washington, DC, area, where
he met a patent attorney who suggested that he go to the George Washington
University Law School and study patent law. While working at GE, Virgil went
to law school at night. After graduating in 1937 and gaining experience as a
patent attorney, Virgil cofounded Woodcock Washburn, a Philadelphia law firm
that specialized in patent law. When it was at its largest, some fifty years after its
founding, the firm had about a hundred patent lawyers, and its clients included

Virgil Woodcock in the 1923 Lakeview High School yearbook.
(Courtesy of the Lake County School District)

Microsoft, DuPont, Johnson & Johnson, the University of Pennsylvania, and Hewlett-Packard. Virgil served as president of the American Patent Law Association and was a member of the US Patent Office Advisory Committee.[8]

Connie, Joycelin, and Virgil were early examples of Lake County youth who not only went on to college but also to graduate and professional schools, which greatly changed their socioeconomic standing and enabled each of them to achieve the American Dream. The inheritability of occupations was much stronger a century ago, when people were less educated and less mobile. Sons and daughters tended to work in the same fields as their parents. In those early years and those that followed, the Daly scholarship had a strong upward pull, moving Lake County youth from ranches and farms to cities throughout the country, where they were lawyers, doctors, teachers, and other professionals.

The children of the very few Lake County professionals also benefitted from the scholarship. Theodore (Ted) Roosevelt Conn, the son of Lake County District Attorney, Lafayette (Lafe) Conn, graduated from Lakeview High School in June of 1926. He wanted to apply for the scholarship, but his father would not allow it as he and Daly were bitter political rivals. Against his father's wishes, Ted applied for and received the scholarship for his senior year at the University of Oregon. Ted went on to law school, then returned to Lakeview to practice law, and, ironically, he served for forty years as the secretary-treasurer of the Daly Fund trustees.

While Ted was at college in the early 1930s, the country's economy was in freefall. The unemployment rate grew to 30 percent, and enrollment at the state's colleges shrank by almost half between 1928 and 1934. Meanwhile, the Daly Fund tried to continue funding scholarships for at least fifteen high school graduates each year as stipulated in Daly's will. For the first time, the trustees used some of the Fund's principal as the accrued interest shrank along with the economy. In 1930, nineteen scholarships were awarded: eighteen in 1931, nineteen in 1932, twenty-three in 1933, and nineteen in 1934; then, in 1935, with municipal bond investments defaulting and underperforming, only eight scholarships were awarded. The next year, 1936, the annual scholarship award was reduced to $500, and sixteen scholarships were awarded.

Mabel Peterson's younger brother, Gene Peterson, was a 1936 high school graduate. After receiving the scholarship in 1924 and majoring in education at the University of Oregon, Mabel returned to Lakeview to teach and was Gene's teacher in his last years of elementary school. Gene told me that Mabel was a tremendous influence on his life, perhaps even more than his parents. She gave him piano lessons, took him on hikes to learn about nature, and emphasized the importance of going to college.

Gene did not really need to be convinced of the importance of college since all six of his older siblings had received a Daly scholarship. It's not surprising that Gene, too, expected to get the scholarship, and when he didn't, he was terribly disappointed. Since he couldn't go to college and didn't want to stay on the farm, he got a job as a bookkeeper at the new bank in town, the First National Bank of Portland, which had purchased the Bank of Lakeview. * According to Myrna (Perry) Bell (LHS 1946), whose family lived on the same tract of land in the New Idaho District, Gene was so accurate he was called Perfect Posting Pete.

Eugene Peterson in the 1944 Purdue yearbook. (Courtesy of the Peterson family)

---

*After the sale of the Bank of Lakeview in 1937, the Lake County Circuit Court took jurisdiction of the Fund and appointed five Lake County residents to serve on the Daly Board of Trustees in place of the Bank of Lakeview directors.

A couple of years later, Gene's older brother, Eric Peterson (LHS 1924), wrote to Gene, encouraging him to attend Purdue University, where Eric had received his PhD in physics and was an instructor of mathematics. Eric urged Gene to live with him and his wife and told him that Purdue forgave tuition for students who stayed on the Distinguished Student List. Gene stayed on the list for all four years and in 1942 received his bachelor's degree in physics, followed by a master's degree in physics at Cal Tech in 1944.

After Cal Tech, Gene worked at the spectroscopy lab at Dow Chemical. He left Dow to work for Hughes Aircraft and was one of several scientists who went on to establish the Santa Barbara Research Center, where he worked for thirty years. Much of Gene's work had to do with navigation through the highly accurate detection of celestial bodies, day or night. Before the widespread use of satellites and GPS, his work was critical to all types of flight and important for both civilian and military applications.

So why didn't Gene get the scholarship? Clearly, he was quite bright and highly motivated. It seems to have been a matter of poor timing and some favoritism. Most of his siblings were older and had graduated from high school before the Depression, when interest earnings for scholarship funds were high, the costs of college were low, and there were relatively few high school graduates. Throughout the 1920s, Oregon public colleges didn't charge tuition for in-state students; they were responsible for course fees, room and board, and textbook expenses only. Following the Depression, state colleges began charging in-state tuition.

When Gene's older brother, Eric, graduated from Lakeview High School in 1924, he was one of twenty-one graduates that year, most of whom received the Daly scholarship. And, in 1924, each recipient received $600 a year—more than the total cost of college attendance. When Gene graduated in 1936, he was one of forty-eight high school graduates. Lakeview had grown, and more students continued on to high school. The effects of the Depression were such that there was only enough money for sixteen scholarships of $500 each.

While 1936 was a particularly challenging year to have graduated from Lakeview High School, Gene's graduating class was the largest to that point, and the Depression depleted the scholarship funds to the lowest ever, a perfect storm of events. At a time when more students wanted to go to college, there were far less scholarship funds available. The pressures came to a head in 1936, when the trustees did not follow the agreed-upon process of selecting students from a list of those who had passed the entrance examination developed by the University of

Oregon and Oregon Agricultural College. The two university presidents wrote to the trustees that "the inclusion of three students whose names were not on the list has been a source of mortification."[9] It seems that those three students were the sons of large account holders at the Bank of Lakeview, whose directors were trustees of the Fund. It did not take long to right the ship. The very next year, the trustees committed to following the process of only selecting students from a list of those who passed the university examination. It was also the year when the Bank of Lakeview was sold to the First National Bank of Portland.

Gene's story had a happy ending, and over time, the same could be said for many of those who did not receive the scholarship but were influenced by it and the Lake County college-going culture. Even in the midst of the Depression, a strong higher-education tradition had been established in Lake County.

The beginnings of the scholarship in the early 1920s coincided with the wild exuberance of the Roaring Twenties, embodying the notion that everything would just get better and better, especially in Lake County where, at a time when so few went to college, almost every Lake County high school graduate who wanted to go, could. One can feel the enthusiasm and pride in this portion of the 1923 annual report that Pearl Hall, the Lake County School superintendent, submitted to the Oregon Superintendent of Public Instruction:

> Since the Bernard Daly educational fund is available there is an incentive for eighth grade pupils to enter high school. Practically 90 per cent of the eighth grade students of last year have entered school this year. Nineteen Lake County high school graduates entered Oregon state institutions this year on scholarships from this fund. The fund amounts to a million dollars. Graduates from all of the Lake County high schools are eligible for scholarships which pay their living expenses up to $600.00.

Having 90 percent of students who complete eighth grade enter high school was extraordinary for the times. The 1920s were about midway through the second great transformation of American schooling: the rise of the public high school. The first transformation was the spread of the common school, free public education through the eighth grade. The third was the growth of college education after World War II, fueled in large part by the GI Bill. In 1920, the median eighteen-year-old in the eastern region of the United States had a 15 percent chance of having completed high school.[10] With almost 90 percent of eighth graders entering high school and most of the graduates going on to college, it was as though Lake County had skipped over the second transformation and went to a time in the future that has yet to be reached by other parts of the country.

But there would be many challenges ahead to assure that Daly's promise to the youth of Lake County would be fulfilled. The growing number of high school graduates, increasing college costs, interest in attending out-of-state and private colleges, and world events were among the issues that Fund trustees would need to consider.

Commissioned Navy officer Jim Ogle. (Courtesy of the Ogle family)

CHAPTER 5

TO WAR AND BACK
1940s–1950s

*Lake County kids enlist. The unexpected consequences of
the GI Bill. An officer on a minesweeper. Liz goes to the state
legislature. A micro-migration from County Cork, Ireland, to
Lake County. Telling the story of the first people to come to
Lake County fourteen thousand years ago. The range wars.
The Daly Fund benefits from exceptional management.*

World events would take many far from Lake County to distant places, where
they would do things well beyond what they might ever have imagined. Jim Ogle
was one who traveled far but then returned to the ranch outside of Lakeview
where he grew up. Jim attended the two-room New Idaho School through the
eighth grade. Although neither of Jim's parents went to college, he was well
aware of the scholarship and the possibility of college as five of his aunts and
uncles were among the first Daly recipients. One of fourteen Lake County high
school graduates to receive the Daly scholarship in 1942, Jim went to Oregon
State College (OSC),* where he majored in agricultural engineering.

After the Japanese attack on Pearl Harbor in December of 1941, America
declared war, first on Japan and then Germany. Young men of college age
enlisted in the military, and many other young men and women went to work
to support the war effort.** The result was a huge drop in college enrollment,
especially among young men. The decrease in enrollment was so great that some

---

*Oregon Agricultural College was renamed Oregon State College in 1932 and then
Oregon State University in 1961.

**During World War II, about four hundred thousand women served with, but not in,
the armed forces. A great many more women worked in factories supporting the war
effort doing what was previously considered man's work. After the War, women were
recognized as a permanent part of the US armed forces with the passage in 1948 of the
Women's Armed Services Integration Act.

colleges were in danger of having to close down during the war. Hardest hit were all-male colleges. When Jim started in agricultural engineering at OSC in the fall of 1942, he was one of 524 students in the School of Agriculture; when he left in 1943, there were only 64. To help prepare much-needed officers and to keep the colleges afloat, special programs for officer training and technical education were established. The Army Specialized Training Program and V-12 Navy College Training Program were announced in December 1942, shortly after Jim arrived on the OSC campus.

Even though OSC was one of the first seven colleges to participate in the Army Specialized Training Program, Jim, who had two uncles and a cousin who had served in the US Navy, was one of the first to join the V-12 program.* He finished out the year at OSC and, as soon spring term ended, was on his way to Purdue, one of the Naval V-12 participating colleges. He continued studies in agricultural engineering along with naval training, beginning with boot camp. Jim was in the navy and college at the same time. He wrote, "We received seaman's pay for that year which wasn't much, but we got our board and room, and I was able to save money. It was as good as herding sheep. We got the weekends off after inspection on Saturday until 8:00 p.m. on Sunday."[1]

After a full year at Purdue, Jim was sent by train to Columbia University in New York City, where a naval officer met him and others who had come from other universities. The officer lined them up and marched them through the city to Columbia, where they had physicals and were issued gray and white officer's uniforms. Jim and the others attended classes during the week, lining up on the parade ground every morning and for bed checks every night. They were at Columbia for four months, changing courses every month. Jim was nineteen when he finished at Columbia and received his commission as a navy ensign. Next he was sent to Cornell.

---

*Between July 1, 1943, and June 30, 1946, the V-12 Program had more than 125,000 participants enrolled in 131 colleges. The course for preofficer candidates who entered as freshmen consisted of four terms of sixteen weeks each. As freshmen, the students were required to take classes in math, English, physics, engineering, naval organization, physical training, and historical backgrounds of the war. After the first year, they specialized in one of five areas: engineering, deck, supply, medical, or dental officers. Students obtained the equivalent of two years of college work in one and one-half years. Graduates of the program were sent to midshipman's school for 120 days, after which they were commissioned ensigns.

Jim spent another four months at Cornell learning about diesel engines and electricity. He then was assigned to the minesweeper USS YMS-294. Jim met the ship at Roi Island, one of the more than a thousand islands that make up the Marshall Islands. He was one of four officers with a twenty-four-man crew. At the time, the YMS-294 was patrolling for submarines. Jim served as the engineering officer and at times also as the minesweeping, communications, and navigation officer.

The YMS-294 was to be part of the planned invasion of Japan, but in August of 1945, atomic bombs were detonated over Hiroshima and Nagasaki. About a week later, the Japanese surrendered to the Allies. Following the surrender, Jim and his ship were assigned to sweep the many channels in the Marshall Islands, looking for Japanese and American mines. There were a few close calls as some of the mines exploded near the ship, but Jim and the ship made it through just fine. In the spring of 1947, the ship got orders to join a convoy in San Diego heading for Panama. After a month in Panama City, they passed through the canal and then up the Atlantic Coast to New Orleans, where the ship was decommissioned with Jim as the commanding officer. When he was discharged after completing his four years of service, Jim was twenty-two.

After his discharge, Jim spent the summer in Lakeview before returning to OSC in the fall of 1947 to finish his degree. While Jim had been away, the Daly trustees approved leaves for Daly students who left college for military service or essential war work. Jim was eligible for his scholarship but, knowing that he had funding from the GI Bill, he told the Fund's administrators that he didn't need the scholarship and wanted to be sure the funds were available to help someone else in the community. Jim was not the first to forgo the scholarship so that others could have it—there were many others. The funding provided by the GI Bill was more generous than the Daly scholarship, which at the time provided $400 each year for four years if the students met the grade and course load requirements. The GI Bill provided up to $500 each year for up to four years of tuition and fees, plus a monthly living stipend of $50 for single men and $75 if married.*

Jim was one of 2.2 million veterans who used the GI Bill to attend college. Colleges that had languished during the depression and shrunk even further in the war years suddenly found their enrollments doubling and, in some cases, tripling. Of the 2.3 million men and women enrolled in US colleges in 1947,

*In 1947, annual tuition and fees for OSC in-state students was $112.50.

about half of them were WW II veterans. The numbers presented an incredible challenge for the nation's colleges—it was described as being like a family that had suddenly inherited a herd of elephants and had to figure out where to put them. Quonset huts, trailers, prefabricated houses, and hastily converted barracks were all used to house the incoming flood of new students. And, despite some educators' concerns, they were very good students. A million and half became professionals: 450,000 engineers; 180,000 doctors, dentists and nurses; 360,000 teachers; 150,000 scientists; 243,000 accountants; and 107,000 lawyers.[2]

In describing the coming of the Knowledge Economy, Peter Drucker wrote, "The postwar WWII GI Bill of Rights—and the enthusiastic response to it on the part of America's veterans—signaled the shift to the knowledge society. Future historians may consider it the most important event of the twentieth century."[3] The astonishing thing about the impact of the GI Bill is that no one saw it coming—the main intent of the Bill was not really about education.

The beginnings of what is now known as the GI Bill go back to the end of WW I, when returning GIs flooded the job market and many were unable to find work. They may not have had jobs, but they did have bonuses in the form of certificates that could not be redeemed until 1945. When the Depression hit, some were still unemployed, and a great many who had jobs lost them. Then, in the spring of 1932, during the worst year of the Depression, Walter W. Waters, a WW I veteran from Portland, Oregon, led a couple of hundred veterans on a three-thousand-mile trek to Washington, DC, to lobby Congress and demonstrate for immediate payment of their bonuses. As they walked and hitched rides on trains, their numbers grew to about twenty thousand veterans, many with families in tow. When they arrived in D.C., they set up camps around the city and made daily walks to the Capitol for rallies. Shortly after Congress refused to grant the bonus payments, US troops led by General Douglas MacArthur drove the veterans from their campsites and burned their makeshift dwellings. In the violent clash, hundreds were injured, and two WW I veterans were shot and later died from their wounds.[4]

The events echoed through time, contributing to Roosevelt's sweeping victory over Hoover and, a decade later, to the passage of a Bill intended to ease the transition of WW II veterans into the labor market. The Servicemen's Readjustment Act of 1944, as it was titled, barely squeaked through committee before easily passing the Senate and House. The college-for-all veterans clause was really an add-on; the main feature of the Bill was a guarantee of twenty dollars a week in unemployment benefits for a year, which became known as the "52–20 Club." Most people thought only a small number of veterans would take advantage of the offer to go to college. Experts predicted 8 to 12 percent–they were wrong. More than half of the fifteen million veterans used the educational benefits–more than two million for college and the rest for vocational training, adult education, and the completion of high school.*

Among the millions who benefited was my father. He went into the army straight out of high school. The first in his family to be born in this country and the first to go to college, he broke new ground. Unlike Jim, he had no family history of college, but thanks to the GI Bill, he created that history for me. After finishing his undergraduate degree with the support of the GI Bill, he kept going, completing a master's and doctorate. After working as a machinist after the war, he began a successful career as a professor in the College of Education at the University of Illinois. I often tell people that my parents did the heavy lifting–I've just followed along the path they made.

Our family wasn't the only one that was changed by the GI Bill. The WW II veterans who experienced the benefits of college expected their children to follow in their footsteps. College became more familiar to Americans and more accessible. The third major educational transformation, higher education, was well underway. In 1940, about 9 percent of eighteen- to twenty-four-year-olds were in college; in 1950, that number had increased to 15 percent. That rate of growth would continue in the decades to come.

Jim finished his degree in the spring of 1948 and then married Dorothy Withers, also an OSC graduate and Daly scholarship recipient from nearby Paisley. Jim and Dorothy returned to the family ranch west of Lakeview, where they raised three girls, all of whom received Daly scholarships and graduated from OSU. Some fifty years later, while serving as the OSU Dean of Education, I would meet the oldest of those daughters, Sue (Ogle) Densmore (LHS 1967), who invited me to her parents' ranch, where I met Jim and Dorothy and learned about their experiences.

---

*Of the 15.75 million WW II veterans: 8.3 million (52 percent) received unemployment benefits (readjustment allowances); about 7.8 million (a little less than half) received educational or training benefits for college, high school, or vocational training; and 4 million (25 percent) took advantage of VA-guaranteed loans to finance a home, farm, or business. In all, about 80 percent of veterans participated in one or more of the programs.

The Ogle sisters: Sara (Ogle) Lea, Martha (Ogle) Powell, and Sue (Ogle) Densmore. (Courtesy of the Ogle family)

Back in Lakeview, Jim and Dorothy ran a dairy and sold bred heifers. In addition to the ranch, Jim was deeply involved in his community, serving as county commissioner, chamber of commerce president, and president of the Lake County Historical Society. A historian and writer, Jim was coeditor of *Lake County History: The First 100 Years*[5] and, with Paiute Snake Tribe descendant Clayton Chocktoot, coauthored *Fort Rock and Paisley Cave Descendants*,[6] telling the story of the first people to come to Lake County more than fourteen thousand years earlier.*

Just as Jim Ogle was leaving the OSC campus for Purdue in 1943, Liz Nelson, another Daly recipient, was arriving. Liz grew up south of Lakeview near Goose Lake, where her grandfather, David Hartzog, settled on a homestead in 1875. Active in the formation of Lake County and Lakeview, Hartzog was a judge of the election that established Lakeview as the county seat, was a juror of the first circuit court in Lakeview, and served as the Lake County deputy sheriff. His

---

*Research by University of Oregon archaeologist Dennis Jenkins shows that radiocarbon-dated human feces found in Paisley Caves are 14,300 years old, predating previous findings from Clovis, New Mexico, by more than three thousand years. It is thought that some of the very first humans to inhabit America traveled by foot from Asia across the land bridge to Lake County where they sought refuge in the Paisley Caves.

daughter (Liz's mother), Delphia Hartzog, was a 1916 OAC graduate, one of very few from Lake County to have gone to college before the Daly scholarship.

In 1943, when Liz went to college, OSC was celebrating its seventy-fifth anniversary. Enrollment was more than four thousand, with about fourteen hundred students enrolled in the Army Specialized Training Program. The remaining students were mostly women, and one of them was Liz.

In the spring of her first year at OSC, Liz was part of a weeding crew sent to a nearby farm owned by the VanLeeuwen family. While weeding onions, she met one of the sons, George VanLeeuwen. He was impressed that she could keep up with him. They married in 1947, just after she graduated, and together managed a family farm in the Irish Bend area along the Willamette River. Over time, the farm evolved from row crops to wheat and grass seed. Although busy raising a young family and helping with the farm, Liz became involved with groups advocating for farmers. She started off as a volunteer for the Oregon Farm Bureau, was a founding member of the Oregon Women for Agriculture, and had a weekly *Farm Report* radio program. Her work with agricultural groups resulted in her being drafted as a write-in for the 1974 Republican primary for the state legislature. Though she wasn't elected, she ran again in 1978 and lost, then won in 1980 on her third run.

Liz brought more to the state capital than the dishpan she used as a briefcase to carry her papers, reports, and newspaper clippings. She also brought steadfast support for the interests of farmers, a persistent work ethic, and a strongly held position on a controversial issue. For decades, grass seed farmers, including Liz and her husband, burned their fields after the harvest to control weeds, remove leftover straw, and destroy diseases. A growing population in the Willamette Valley, along with greater awareness of environmental issues, led to more and more complaints about air pollution caused by the burning. In August of 1969, Governor McCall issued a temporary ban on field burning. In response, Liz and others organized Oregon Women in Agriculture to argue against the ban and advocate for field burning. Support for controlled field burning was a key position in each of Liz's early campaigns. It was a hotly debated topic in the legislature for years; then, in 1988, a field burn got out of control, and the smoke caused poor visibility that resulted in a multicar pileup on Interstate 5 that killed seven people and injured thirty. It was a tipping point. The tide had turned, and legislators passed stricter regulations on burning. Then in 1991, the state mandated a phaseout of almost all field burning.

By that time, Liz had become embroiled in an even bigger environmental issue, fighting in support of logging against the preservation of the spotted owl and its natural old-growth habitat. Her district and much of Oregon were mired in a severe economic recession caused in large part by a downturn in construction and the corresponding loss of jobs in the timber industry. Even more losses appeared imminent as environmental groups lobbied to have the northern spotted owl declared an endangered species, which would severely limit logging of old-growth timber. It was an all-out battle between the timber industry and the environmentalists, and Liz was a leader for timber interests. She testified at congressional hearings, wrote editorials, and responded to claims by environmentalists, arguing that there were more spotted owls than had been counted and that the existing 4.5 million acres of old-growth forest already set aside in Oregon and Washington was plenty.* Once again, Liz found herself fighting a losing battle. In June 1990, the northern spotted owl was declared a threatened species, and timber companies were required to leave at least 40 percent of the old-growth forests intact within a 1.3-mile radius of any spotted owl activity. Mills closed, and the Oregon economy lagged behind the rest of the country. Liz kept fighting but the die was cast. The Oregon timber industry never fully recovered.**

While those were losing efforts, she was on the winning side in keeping the state from condemning farm land to create a giant park along both sides of the Willamette River from Portland to Eugene. Also, her efforts to keep Oregon universities and community colleges on the quarter system rather than semesters were successful.*** Win or lose, she was persistent and always on the side of farmers.

Liz was ninety-three when I met her on the family farm, which her son now manages. Her legislative career had ended more than twenty years earlier, yet she was still an activist, speaking out in support of farmers. While there are far

---

*Liz told everyone who would listen that the amount of set-aside old-growth timber was enough for a two-mile-wide strip from Portland, Oregon, to New York City.

**Ironically, the preservation of the spotted owl and corresponding end to the cutting of old-growth timber led to a boom in timber harvests and mill operations in Lake County as there was less available timber in the Willamette Valley.

*** The quarter system was an important issue to farmers and others who employ college students in the late summer for harvesting, food processing, and forestry.

fewer farmers today than during her grandfather's time, the productivity and importance of farming and agriculture has never been higher. Both Liz and Jim followed their parents into farming and ranching, but fewer and fewer of those who came after them would be able to do so.

In her 90s, Liz continues to advocate for farmers. (Courtesy of the VanLeeuwen family)

Dan Dunham (left) and Jim Lynch in the 1954 Lakeview High School Yearbook. (Courtesy of the Lake County School District)

Two talented kids graduated from Lakeview High School in 1954. One grew up on a farm, the other on a ranch; one went to Oregon State College, the other to the University of Oregon; one became a Democrat, the other a Republican. One would be the first to tell me about the Daly scholarship; the other would help me get started on the research. For a time, they both worked in Washington, DC, in service of their country, and both returned to Oregon, one to Lakeview and the other to the university community of Corvallis, where he received all three of his degrees.

Dan Dunham's family moved to Lake County in 1939. His father thought it was like Wyoming, where he had grown up, and although neither he nor his wife had gone to college, he hoped that the Daly scholarship would make it possible for their four kids to go. Dan grew up working on the family farm. As one might expect, agriculture was his favorite high school class, and he was actively involved in the local chapter of the Future Farmers of America (FFA). But he had interests well beyond agriculture. He played the tuba in the band, acted in every school play, was on the student council, and was the announcer for the high school basketball games. A talented, well-spoken kid, he won the state FFA public speaking award and, in the spring of his senior year, he was elected state

FFA president. When he graduated, he was one of fifteen to get the Daly scholarship. His older sister had received it before him, and he remembers going to see the list posted on the window of Ted Conn's law office each year to see who got it and who didn't.

In the fall of 1954, he went to OSC as an agriculture major but was still quite busy as state FFA president, and his grades suffered. His fall term GPA was below the 2.2 requirement for freshmen that had just been implemented at the June 1954 trustee meeting.* He hadn't even been home for a week during the Christmas vacation when he got a call summoning him to Ted Conn's law office. Ted asked Dan what was going on with his grades, knowing that his GPA was below the required average. When Dan said that he was busy with FFA duties, Ted told him to quit FFA and concentrate on school. Dan said he couldn't quit, so, with Ted's support, he took a leave of absence for winter term. That's the way it worked. Not only was it a small town, with everyone seemingly knowing everyone else's business, but Ted Conn, secretary-treasurer of the Daly trustees, received the term grades for every Daly student from the state colleges—and the students all knew that.

Dan did go back to OSC for spring term and did much better but was then elected national FFA president and had to take another leave for the entire 1955–56 academic year to fulfill his FFA duties. Dan returned to college in the fall of 1957, but he was drafted the following fall. After two years in the military as an assistant chaplain, he finally graduated in 1962 in agriculture education from Oregon State University (OSU).**

Given his experiences in serving as state and then national FFA president, one might think that Dan won every election he entered. Not so. Back at Lakeview High School, he had run for student body president and lost in a close race to Jim Lynch, another talented Lakeview kid who lived in town during the school

---

*At the annual meeting of the Daly trustees on June 26, 1954, the trustees established GPA requirements of 2.2 for freshmen and 2.5 for juniors. Student GPAs could be below the required average for any single term, but the overall GPA for the year would have be at or above the required average for the scholarship to be renewed the next year. At that meeting, the trustees also established the requirement that all Daly students complete a minimum of fifteen quarter-hour credits each academic term, which would enable the students to complete degrees in four years.

**Dan started at Oregon State College (OSC) in the fall of 1954 and graduated from Oregon State University (OSU) in the spring of 1962 after the name changed in 1961.

year and on the family ranch in Plush during the summer. Jim's family, on both his mother's and father's sides, had come to Lake County from Ireland in the late 1800s. Jim's maternal great-grandfather, Phillip Kane Barry, was one of four Barry brothers who left the Duhallow region of County Cork in Ireland, going first to California, where they were sheepherders, and then in the 1880s to Lake County, where at the time there were no restrictions on grazing on the public lands. The Barry brothers began a micro-migration from their Irish home in Duhallow to Lake County that continued for almost seventy years.

One of the first to follow the Barrys was Philip Lynch, from Jim's father's side of the family. Each year a few young Irishmen from Duhallow would make the long trip by ship and then train to Lake County, where they became sheep-herders. The terms of the arrangement were that the immigrants (greenhorns) were expected to work for their sponsors for a year or two as sheepherders, after which they were given sheep they could mark with their own brands. After a few years, they could leave their sponsors and set up their own operations, even without owning much land. As these men established their own herds, they sent word back to Ireland for their brothers and other relatives to come and work for them. Each spring in the early 1900s, about ten would gather at the Cork County Newmarket railway station for the train to Queenstown, where a tender took them out to the ship on which, cramped into the third-class section, they would cross the Atlantic in seven to ten days. When they arrived in New York, they had another seven to ten days of train travel to reach Lakeview. It's said that before leaving Duhallow, they were told, "Don't stop in the United States but keep going until you get to the Barry Ranch in Plush; you'll be safe there."[7]

As the number of sheepherders increased, so did the number of sheep. Before 1880, there were virtually no sheep in eastern Oregon; by 1900, the more than 2.5 million sheep on the slopes of eastern Oregon's grazing lands led to con-flicts with cattlemen. The grazing lands that had seemed limitless were unable to regenerate themselves because of overgrazing. It was a tragedy of the commons, the ranching equivalent of the Dust Bowl. While the cattle ate only the grass, leaving the weeds to hold down the topsoil and allowing the grass to regrow, the sheep ate everything. In response to the overgrazing and resulting range wars, the Taylor Grazing Act was passed in 1934, permitting only those with a home ranch to lease federal lands for grazing. The cattlemen and the sheepmen adjusted by purchasing land and forming corporations. That is what the Barrys and others from Ireland did, and over time they switched from sheep to cattle.

In the summer of 1953, before Jim Lynch's senior year at Lakeview High School, the Lynch Ranch hired an unlikely ranch hand. David Maxey had just finished his freshman year at Harvard and traveled cross-country to Lake County to work on a ranch. By chance, he found his way to the Lynch ranch. I met David in Philadelphia in 2019 when he was eighty-five, yet he recalled that summer as though it had just happened. Here's his vivid description of the 1953 ranch as he remembers it:

> The Lynch ranch was of four parts. The first was the JJ, the house of some age, where the Lynch family spent the summer when they weren't in town. The JJ, the Lynch brand, when used as a location marker, included irrigated hay fields on both sides of Honey Creek that produced premium alfalfa hay which, once cut, was stacked in several fenced-in stack yards. The stacks looked very much like the old-fashioned loaf of bread after it came out of the oven.
>
> The second part was the 27, named because it was in Section 27 east of the JJ. It was headquarters for the ranch operation. In the 27 Yard were located the cookhouse, the bunkhouse, the shop, the tack room, and the corral, together with tractors and other equipment. The ranch day began and ended at the 27. Like the JJ, the 27 also had adjoining hayfields, more in number than the JJ, and usually mowed after the JJ.
>
> The third part of the ranch was the Swamp, located north of the 27. Con Lynch bought it from the Bank of the Willows which must have foreclosed on this large area of marshy land that dried out enough in the summer so that the haying crew could move in and cut the wild hay found there. It was, I confess, the high point of my time on the haying crew when at last we got to the Swamp, usually around the Fourth of July, and where we finished up at about Labor Day, which coincided with Roundup in Lakeview.
>
> In all these three hayfield areas Lynch cattle wintered.
>
> The fourth part requires backtracking to Camas, a valley that opens up about halfway between Lakeview and Plush. It was picture-perfect in my view of it. Lynch cattle taken off the open range would summer there. Brandings took place in Camas, and they were events to anticipate.
>
> The Lynch ranch as other ranches in Plush put their cattle out on the open range in the spring and summer. One lesson I learned early

was to realize that the relationship between the BLM and the Forest Service, on the one hand, and the ranching community, on the other, was not always a cordial one.

Jim was a cowboy, a buckaroo, at heart, but he also worked on the haying crew. He knew the ranching business backward and forward. He was a great friend for me in those summer months.

David returned the next summer and the next, deepening his affection for the Warner Valley and his friendship with Jim. After graduation, David went on to Harvard Law School, and Jim went to the University of Oregon in 1954. Jim may have been, as David said, a cowboy and a buckaroo, but he did very well at the University of Oregon, where he won the Koyl Cup, presented to the most all-round man in the junior class, and the Quartermaster Association Award, given to only ten ROTC cadets in the United States. Jim's senior year was quite eventful. As student body president, he traveled with the University of Oregon football team to the Rose Bowl in Pasadena; then, in May of 1958, he introduced John F. Kennedy, who spoke at the university student union building. It may have been awkward for Jim. He was a staunch Republican, as were all his family members, but all the Lynches were also fiercely proud of their Irish Catholic heritage.

After graduation, Jim went on to the University of Oregon law school, finishing in 1961 after having won the Paul Patterson Fellowship in Law and Public Service, which was awarded each year to the senior law student who best exemplified integrity, leadership, and public service. After law school, Jim served two years with the Judge Advocate Corps in Washington, DC, where he had one final encounter with President Kennedy; Jim's unit had the responsibility of handling parking at Kennedy's funeral, directing the limos of attending world leaders.

While Jim was completing his service with the Judge Advocate Corps, Dan Dunham was teaching vocational agriculture in Drain, Oregon, a community of about a thousand in southwest Oregon. Then in 1965, Dan went to the larger community of Lebanon, where he again started new vocational agriculture and FFA programs. In 1970, after completing his doctorate in education at OSU, Dan worked at the Oregon Department of Education before moving to Maryland, where he was the state director of vocational education. In 1978, he was appointed deputy commissioner for vocational and adult education in the US Office of Education. In 1980, President Jimmy Carter appointed Dan as the first assistant secretary of education for that program in the newly formed US Department of Education.

Dan was able to finance his graduate education through National Defense Education Act (NDEA) loans. The passage of NDEA was influenced by the successful launch of the Sputnik satellite in 1957 and the general sense that the United States was falling behind the Soviet Union in technology and science. On the very day that Sputnik first orbited the earth, Stewart McClure, chief clerk of the Senate's Education and Labor Committee, sent a memo to his chairman, Alabama Democrat Lister Hill, suggesting that if he called the education bill he had been trying to pass a defense bill, it might pass. It did pass, and the NDEA established the precedent of the federal government loaning money for college. Although aimed primarily at science, mathematics, and foreign languages, the act also helped expand college libraries and other services for all students. The funding began in 1958 and was increased over the next several years. Like the GI Bill, the results were dramatic: in 1960, there were 3.6 million students in college, and by 1970, there were 7.5 million. One of those students was Dan, who told me that he wrote monthly checks to pay off the low-interest NDEA loans. He wrote the last check the very month he began work as the deputy commissioner in 1979.

Dan left the US Department of Education in 1980, shortly after the beginning of President Reagan's first term, and moved to Ohio State University, where he was the associate director of the National Center for Research in Vocational Education. In 1983, Dan returned to Oregon to join the faculty of the College of Education at Oregon State University. That's where I met Dan and first learned about the Daly scholarship. Dan's story of the scholarship stuck with me, and over time I met a surprising number of people from Lakeview, including Jim and Dorothy Ogle's daughter, Sue (Ogle) Densmore. Twenty-five years after Dan and I first met, I told him that I wanted to do research on the impact of the Fund. He suggested I go to Lakeview and talk with Jim Lynch, who was then the Fund's secretary-treasurer.

After completing his Army service in the Judge Advocate Corps in 1963, Jim returned to Lakeview to join Ted Conn's law practice. As a small-town lawyer, Jim had to be a generalist—some business law, estate planning, family law, criminal defense, and municipal law—a little bit of everything, which was quite different from his friend David Maxey, who had a distinguished career with a large

Philadelphia law firm specializing in commercial real estate law. In comparison with big-city lawyers, Jim had a lot of direct client interactions. It seemed he knew everyone in town, and they trusted him with their private affairs. In addition to the law practice, Jim assisted Ted, who still served as secretary-treasurer for the Daly trustees. In the 1970s, Jim would take over as secretary-treasurer and, as Ted did before him, would serve the Board of Trustees for about forty years.

Following Dan Dunham's advice, I went to Lakeview and met with Jim, who patiently told me about the scholarship and its history. He encouraged me to contact some of the recipients and gave me a list of the almost two thousand who had been awarded the scholarship since 1922. He made a point of telling me that these were the selectees, not necessarily recipients; some of the selectees had declined the scholarship because their families had enough money for them to go to college, and they knew someone else in the community could use it more. It wasn't until a decade later, after Jim had died, when I spoke with Jim's sister Breda, also a Daly selectee, and learned that Jim and Breda had both declined the scholarship so that others might have it.

The growth of higher education between 1940 and 1960 was extraordinary. Fueled by the GI Bill and then the NDEA, college enrollments grew from one and a half million in 1940 to over four million in 1960. And the number of colleges grew from about eight hundred in 1940 to more than twenty-five hundred in 1960. The cost of tuition also increased. At Oregon State University, annual tuition and fees rose from $102 in 1940 to $370 in 1960. The Daly scholarship, which provided $600 and covered all costs when it was first awarded in 1922, provided $400 in 1940, then back to $600 in 1960.*

In 1960, about 25 percent of all US eighteen- to twenty-four-year-olds were in college, but in Lake County, more than half of the high school graduates went to college. In the years to come, this would lead the Daly Fund trustees to consider several issues, including standardized methods for selecting recipients, leaves of absence for study-abroad programs, and support for attending community colleges and eventually web-based programs.

---

*Total estimated costs at OSU in 1960 (including tuition, fees, room and board, books, and miscellaneous) was $1,320.

CHAPTER 6

THE TIMES THEY ARE
A-CHANGIN'
1960s–1970s

*From Dachau to Lakeview and then West Point. Lake
County kids compete with the best and the brightest. An
unlikely molecular biologist. The family plan. Generosity
leads to more generosity. Four generations of pharmacists.
Out of the woods. Becoming a citizen in Lakeview.*

Everyone came from somewhere else: those who walked across the land bridge
from Asia more than fourteen thousand years ago; Bernard Daly from Ireland
by way of Selma, Alabama; the Barry brothers and the many Irish who followed
them; and the Okies escaping the Dust Bowl—all found their way to Lake County
in search of a better life. One who traveled a long distance to find a home in Lake
County was Arpad Kovacsy.

Arpad was only two when he and his family were taken from their home in
Hungary in 1944 and imprisoned at Dachau because Arpad's father was a government official who would not collaborate with the occupying Nazis.*When
Dachau was liberated in April 1945, Arpad and his family were among the
eleven million refugees in Europe. With the help of the International Refugee
Organization and the Presbyterian Churches of America, Arpad's family found
a home in America in, of all places, Lakeview, Oregon, where Dan Dunham's
family was their sponsor.

---

*Hungary was allied with the Axis powers at the beginning of World War II, but as
losses mounted, the Hungarian government began secret negotiations with the Allies
in 1943. Learning of the negotiations, Germany occupied Hungary in March 1944. In
the early months of the occupation, about half a million Hungarian Jews were sent to
concentration camps, most to Auschwitz. Some Hungarian political figures and their
families (including Arpad's family) were sent to Dachau.

The Kovacsy family lived with the Dunhams for several years in the early 1950s. Arpad's father helped out on the farm and ranch until he found work as a janitor at the county courthouse and moved the family into their own home. Arpad's father made the adjustment from having been a wealthy Hungarian government official who could trace his noble lineage to the mid-1600s to a janitor in Lakeview, where he played cards with the courthouse judges and lawyers and felt a kinship with many of the Irish, who were also immigrants fresh off the boat. Lakeview became home.

Jim Clinton, who would become Arpad's best friend, remembers when Arpad joined his first-grade class toward the end of the school year. Arpad, who hardly spoke English, went to summer school to learn English and from then on was an excellent student. By the end of elementary school, Arpad, Jim, and all of their friends knew about the Daly scholarship and its importance; most of their families did not have money for college. Arpad and Jim both had happy memories of their childhood in Lakeview. They made mazes out of cardboard boxes in the basement of the courthouse. Then there was the time they brewed some sort of concoction and stored it in the attic in Jim's house. After some particularly warm weather, there was an explosion. It seems that Jim, who would later become a physicist, had an early interest in science.

About the time Arpad started junior high school, he began thinking about West Point. He remembered an American Army officer, a West Point grad, who had helped to liberate Dachau and befriended his family. Arpad's interest in West Point motivated him to get good grades and stay near the top of the class. In the summer between eighth and ninth grade, he went to a military academy in Minnesota to see how he would do in a military environment. At the end of his junior year, he took the required physical and academic tests; at the beginning of his senior year, Arpad became the first Lake County student to be nominated for West Point.*

The process to get into West Point was highly competitive, and the four-year West Point experience was even more so. Arpad was well prepared for academic competition. He was a bright kid and had grown up in a healthy, competitive academic environment—his friends wanted to excel, and the Lakeview teachers believed all, or almost all, of the kids would go on to college. It had been

---

*Arpad is grateful to Congressman Al Ullman, who represented Oregon's Second Congressional District from 1957 to 1981; he made appointments to West Point based primarily on merit rather than political favor.

forty years since the scholarship was created, and a college-going culture had taken hold in Lake County. In the early 1960s, about a quarter of all eighteen-to twenty-four-year-olds in America went to college, but well more than half of Arpad's graduating class went on to college. It was as though Lakeview High School was a college prep school.

Arpad and his friend Jim Clinton were among the top students in their class, especially in math and science. While Arpad went to West Point, Jim, who was one of the nineteen Daly scholarship recipients that year, went to the University of Oregon, where he majored in physics. Jim's high school girlfriend, Gail Robin, a 1964 graduate, also received the Daly scholarship but went to Oregon State University. Reflecting on that time, Gail told me that she wasn't particularly ambitious. Neither of her parents or sisters had gone to college, and she was not sure what to study. As did many women of her generation, she majored in elementary education, more by default than choice, but before the year was over, she transferred to the University of Oregon, where Jim was in his senior year. They married and together moved to southern California, where Jim had a graduate assistantship in physics at the newly established University of California San Diego (UCSD).* It was an exciting time to be in the sciences at UCSD; the whole campus was focused on science, and there were two Nobel Prize winners on the same floor where Jim had a graduate student office. Jim completed his master's and doctoral degrees at UCSD and then post-doc studies at Scripps, all focusing on solid-state physics and thin-film materials.

Meanwhile, Gail was forced to choose from biology, math, or physics—the only undergraduate majors offered in the early years at UCSD. She picked biology but wasn't putting much effort into her studies, and it showed. She was getting Cs and felt she was flailing until she started a work-study project on transfer ribonucleic acid (RNA) in a biomedical research lab at Scripps Clinic. Working in the lab on an actual project changed everything. She fell in love with molecular research and from then on got all As. In the work-study program for three years, she worked twenty hours a week during the academic year and full time in the summers. It was an exhilarating time; it seemed that every UCSD lab was doing

---

*University of California San Diego was originally planned to be a graduate and research institution, providing instruction in the sciences, mathematics, and engineering. As such, it was designed from the top down in terms of research emphasis. Over time it became a broad-based institution but maintained strength in the sciences, with twenty-five Nobel Laureates in the first fifty years of its history.

cutting-edge research. Jim Allison, another work-study student in the same lab, went on to receive the 2018 Nobel Prize for developing an effective new way to attack cancer by treating the immune system rather than the cancerous tumor.

After finishing her undergraduate degree, Gail went on to the UCSD graduate program, where she researched animal viruses. That led to a postdoctoral appointment at Harvard Medical School, where Gail continued her research on viruses and began work on the identification of a molecular marker that showed potential for predicting outcomes of breast cancer. After leaving Harvard, Gail joined the faculty at the Louisiana State University Medical Center and then moved to Oregon Health Sciences University, where she headed a research team that identified a protein fragment that helps predict outcomes from breast cancer. That protein fragment, P95 HER-2, which was first touted as a prognostic marker, is now useful in cancer treatments.

Gail is an example of someone from Lake County who probably would not have gone to college if it were not for the Daly scholarship. Like a tide that raises all boats, the Daly scholarship and the emerging college-going culture in Lake County had an especially strong impact on first-generation college students such as Gail, getting them to college where their talent could be realized.

In many ways, Gail's timing was especially fortunate—she was in the right place at the right time. She showed up at UCSD when it was first established and the only majors were in the sciences. Her pivotal work-study position was available because of the passage of the Higher Education Act (HEA) in 1965. Part of President Lyndon Johnson's Great Society Agenda, it included funding for student loans, grants, and work-study positions for college students. The 1965 HEA, like the GI Bill, was misjudged by the experts who greatly underestimated both the number of students who would assume loans and the amount of money they would borrow. The result has been a two-sided legacy: greater access to college and greater student debt.

While in graduate school, Gail and Jim divorced; each finished a doctorate and went on to postdoctoral studies and remarkable careers. Jim had a postdoc position at Scripps Institution of Oceanography, where he did research in physics, chemistry, and solar energy. He then founded a high-tech company doing aerospace research and development for NASA and other government agencies. In 1995, Jim moved his R&D lab to Bend, Oregon, where he pursued aerospace, medical device, and renewable energy projects. When the area where he lived was annexed into the city, and developers planned a large housing project for the nearby elk reserve property, Jim became involved in local politics. He was elected to twelve years on the Bend City Council, including serving as Bend's mayor from 2012 to 2016. Bend's population grew from twenty thousand in 1990 to about a hundred thousand in 2020, causing civic discord and growth-management challenges. Jim found his science background helpful in addressing the complex issues of a rapidly growing city.[1]

At West Point in the early 1960s, Arpad found that he could compete with the very best in his class. He and the other cadets received a general education without a specific major, although there was a clear emphasis on math and the sciences. The intent was to prepare officers with versatility so they could succeed in a variety of areas after graduation. They learned how to lead others, solve complex problems, use time and resources wisely, and "choose the harder right over the easier wrong." Arpad did well in his classes; he especially liked math and history and was among the first five cadets at West Point ever to be commissioned in military intelligence.

After graduation, Arpad wanted to serve in Vietnam, but at the time, West Point grads were not sent to Vietnam because so many had lost their lives in those early years of fighting. Enthusiastic and determined, Arpad requested assignment to Korea, where he was then able to transfer to Vietnam and serve two tours of duty. After Vietnam, he was in charge of communications for NATO European Headquarters and then, at twenty-six, he headed a specialized 290-person unit responsible for an advanced telecommunications unit in Southeast Asia. After leaving the service, Arpad went to law school at Duke, then was appointed to a five-year term on the Postal Rate Commission during the Carter Administration. In the 1980s, Arpad was president and CEO of TCOM Systems; he then founded INTEGRAM, a leader in computer-generated direct mail, which grew rapidly and was named an Inc. 500 Company.

Arpad, Jim, and Gail were kids during the 1950s. They had duck-and-cover drills in elementary school during the height of the Cold War, and when they went to college in the sixties, they found themselves in the midst of campus unrest and student protests. For the kids from Lake County, it must have felt like whiplash. Lake County was politically conservative, and college campuses (except for West Point and some others) were becoming more political and increasingly liberal. They were a part of the baby boomers who went to college in record numbers. Between 1960 and 1972, forty-five million youth turned eighteen, and more than ever before went to college. In 1960, there were three million students in college; at the end of the decade, there were about ten million.[2]

On college campuses throughout the country, it was a culturally and politically disruptive and polarizing time. Students, whether morally opposed to the Vietnam War or afraid of losing their draft deferments, joined faculty in antiwar protests and demonstrations in support of free speech. By the end of the 1960s, many campuses were seen as centers of opposition to American foreign policies; at the same time, millions of working-class Americans who had not gone to college turned against activist universities. Friends and family found themselves on opposite sides of arguments.

Reflecting on those times, Jim Clinton said:

> When I was a kid, I think the majority of Lake County residents were Democrats, many with strong memories of what FDR did for the country. Eastern Oregon was represented by a Democrat, Al Ullman. The shift to conservatism started with the friction between the traditional values of a place like Lakeview and the liberal hippie culture that seemed to be taking over the college campuses and big cities. Sadly, this divide between those who left and those who remained has deepened over the years. The rift could be clearly seen at our 50th class reunion.

The 1960s gave way to the '70s, and the Vietnam War ended, but the memories lingered, and they would echo through time.

The first European settlers called the region the District of Lakes. The lakes were once large and deep but have been drying for more than eleven thousand years, and many are now alkaline or dry. Next to one of them, Alkali Lake about sixty miles north of Lakeview, is a stark reminder of the Vietnam War. Inside barbed-wire fencing is a patch of desert where 25,513 barrels containing more than a million gallons of pesticide, commonly known as Agent Orange, are buried. In 1976, when the barrels started to leak, bulldozers were used to crush the barrels and push them into unlined trenches. The groundwater near the site is now contaminated, and water samples are the color of cherry Kool-Aid.[3] Echoes through time.

Jim, Gail, and Arpad all went on to complete graduate and professional degrees. While it was extraordinary for the time, it was not uncommon for the kids from Lake County. Continuing on to graduate and professional studies became so common for youth from Lake County that, following Bernard Daly's example, Burt Snyder created a scholarship for graduate education.

Snyder came to Lakeview from Plush in the early 1900s and went to work at Thornton's Drugstore. He wanted to become a pharmacist, and Mr. Thornton helped him enroll in a correspondence course. When he completed the course, Burt traveled to Portland in 1910 to take the apprentice pharmacist exam. The journey may have been harder than the exam. It took him two days by stage to Klamath Falls and then another day and a half to Portland by train. He got his license and returned to Lakeview to work for Vinton Hall and Fred Reynolds, who had bought out Dr. Daly's interest in the pharmacy. In 1912, Snyder bought out Dr. Hall's interest, and the store became known as Snyder and Reynolds.

In 1938, Snyder sold his interest in the drugstore to Clifton Howard and ran for the state legislature. In a campaign statement published in the *Bend Bulletin* that May, Snyder wrote:

> I was born near Lakeview in 1890 and have been here since that time.
> My education is limited to grade and high school. I studied pharmacy
> in the back end of a drug store and was licensed as a registered phar-
> macist upon examination by the state board of pharmacy in 1911.

Snyder won that election, the next one, and the next one, and so on. He served as a member of the Oregon House of Representatives for five terms, from 1939 through 1948. He was a Republican but was so popular that in 1940, he not only won the Republican nomination but also received enough Democratic write-in votes to win the Democratic primary. After serving in the state legislature, Snyder focused his activities on Lakeview, serving on the Bernard Daly Fund board of trustees for many years. When he died in 1964, his will established the Burt Snyder Educational Foundation, which provides scholarships to Lake County youth for graduate or professional studies. This was especially important to Snyder; he had studied pharmacy in the back of a drug store, in the 1950s, pharmacy had become a five-year program requiring an additional year more than was funded by the Daly scholarship. Snyder wanted to make it possible for Lake County students to pursue graduate degrees.

The Burt Snyder graduate scholarship is administered by the Daly trustees and is part of a growing family of scholarships influenced by the Daly scholarship. Others include the Collins McDonald scholarship, which provides scholarships that can be used at out-of-state and private colleges; the Anna Jones scholarship, specifically for students who graduate from Paisley High School; the Ousley scholarship for students from Lake and Klamath counties; and the Jean Tesche scholarship for language study, first awarded in 2018.

Jean Tesche was a 1973 LHS grad who received the Daly scholarship and went to the University of Oregon, where she studied languages, and then to Columbia for an MBA and a PhD in economics and finance. After some university teaching, she worked for the US Treasury, World Bank, and World Health Organization in many countries, including Bosnia, Croatia, Serbia, and Burkina Faso. At the time of our interview, she was working in Cape Town, South Africa. Though Jean lives about as far away from Lakeview as one can, she has attended every one of her class reunions. In 2018, Jean established a scholarship for students from Oregon's small towns who want to study languages. The first recipient was a young man who graduated from Klamath Falls' Mazama High School, where he studied Spanish and German. With the help of Jean's scholarship, he attended OSU, majoring in history and Russian language.

More than half of the population of Lake County lives outside the city of Lakeview. It's a big county, about the size of New Jersey with a lot fewer people. As big as Lake County is, it only has two incorporated towns: Lakeview, the county seat, and Paisley, fifty miles north of Lakeview, with about 250 residents. In addition to Lakeview and Paisley, there are a handful of unincorporated towns that are the home communities for Lake County ranching families. One of those communities is Adel, in Warner Valley, about thirty miles to the east of Lakeview. The town of Adel has a general store, Catholic church, small post office, and two-room school (the Adel School District). These days, the Adel School District teams up with the neighboring Plush School District, twenty miles to the north. Together they typically have about a dozen K–8 students; all of them go to Plush for kindergarten to third grade and then to Adel for fourth to eighth grade. From there, most take the long bus ride to Lakeview for high school and, thanks to the Daly and Collins McDonald scholarships, most go on to college.

In 1948, John Shine was among the last to make the journey from Duhallow in County Cork, Ireland, to Lake County. Sponsored by Philip Kane Barry's son (Philip P. Barry), he settled on 120 acres near Adel. John met his wife, Laura Verling, who was born in Lakeview to parents who had come from Duhallow in the early 1900s. Together they raised six children, all of whom received either the Daly or the Collins McDonald scholarship and went on to college. Raising six kids on a 120-acre ranch was quite a feat. With only a few hundred cows and one payday a year, a lot was riding on the price for cattle and the quality of each year's herd. The calves were born in March and sold in October; then that year's line of credit was paid off and a new one borrowed. Year after year, it was hard work, with not much extra to be had.

John Sr. completed sixth grade in Ireland, and his wife, Laura, went to Armstrong Business College in Berkeley, California. After earning a degree in bookkeeping, she returned to Lakeview, where she and John Sr. were married in 1958. Though neither had gone to a four-year college, they were determined that their kids would do well in school and go to college. The eldest, John Jr., remembers going to the two-room Adel school when there were enough kids for Adel and Plush to each have K–8 schools. There were six in John's class, five boys and a girl. They sat in rows by class and sometimes worked together and sometimes individually or by class.

During much of the 1960s, the Adel teaching staff was a husband-and-wife team, Bob and Shirley Crawford. Shirley taught grades one to three, and Bob taught grades four to eight. In 1966, Bob organized a local science fair and took forty-five people to Portland (the winners and many proud parents) for the Northwest Science Fair at the Oregon Museum of Science and Industry. That year there were 250,000 entries, and fifty-nine gold medals were awarded; the Adel kids won five. Bob coached one more gold winner by mail, Karen Degarmo from Alvord Desert, about a hundred miles east of Adel, where she attended the two-room Fields K–8 school. That year, Bob was named Oregon Middle School Science Teacher of the Year.

Community life in Adel was focused on the school. Everyone participated in school activities. Mary, John's sister, was on the Adel boys' football and basketball teams because there were not enough boys. There were cookouts most Friday evenings at the school; everyone would bring a foil packet and put it in the coals. The Adel kids grew up together, and when they finished eighth grade, they rode together on the little bus for the hour ride each way to and from Lakeview for high school. Mary learned to play poker on that bus. When I asked John, who went on to OSU for college, about the adjustment from little Adel to the much-bigger Corvallis for college, he said, "No, going to OSU wasn't that big of a change, but going to Lakeview High School from Adel—that was big, there were so many kids."

John did get the Collins McDonald scholarship, which operated under the same rules as the Daly scholarship except that the recipients could go to private

John Shine on his ranch.

colleges, out-of-state colleges, or technical schools. John was not sure he would go to college, but his father was adamant, telling him that if he went, then his brothers and sisters would follow him.

John went to OSU, where he majored in agricultural economics. Thinking he might follow in the footsteps of his Uncle Frank, who was a banker, John accepted an internship with a bank but found it boring; instead, he took a job at Ralston Purina, where he worked in animal feed sales. After seven years at Ralston Purina, he started his own pet food company. It grew from three employees to more than seven hundred in 2010, when he sold it to a private equity firm. After the sale, John and his family moved back to Lakeview and bought the ranch west of town that had been in his mother's family. On about five thousand acres, John has an RV Park and also provides summer grazing for local ranchers from spring until about Thanksgiving, when they return to their home ranch and are fed hay. It's a little like a kennel for cows—a dollar-fifty a day for grazing and care for a mature cow and her calf.

Among the local ranchers who bring their cattle to the ranch for summer grazing is John's youngest brother, George, who also received the Collins McDonald scholarship and studied agriculture at OSU. George is the only one of the six who went back to Lakeview after college and went into ranching. Pat, a 1977 graduate, received the Daly scholarship, studied computer programming at OSU, and works as a computer programmer in the Portland area. Mary, a 1979 graduate, also received the Daly scholarship, went to OSU, and then worked in pharmaceutical sales in the Seattle area. Bill, a 1980 graduate, received the Collins McDonald scholarship; he also studied agriculture at OSU and then worked at Ralston Purina. Julie, a 1983 graduate and Daly recipient, was a food science major at OSU and then worked at Hewlett-Packard in Boise, Idaho. All six of the Shine kids graduated in four years.

There were many Lake County families to have all the kids get scholarships. Among them is the Howard family of Howard's Drug Store, the beginnings of which go all the way back to the 1880s and Bernard Daly. As was common in that time, Daly provided a pharmacy as part of his medical office.* By the end of the 1800s, Daly and Hall moved the pharmacy into a new building built by Daly, who was becoming Lakeview's largest property owner. In 1909, Vinton Hall and young Fred Reynolds bought out Daly's interest and opened Hall and Reynolds Drugs. When Burt Snyder received his pharmacist license, he went to work for Hall and Reynolds and, in 1912, bought out Vinton Hall's interest. The sign was changed to Snyder and Reynolds. Young Clifton Howard, who worked as a clerk in the store, graduated from Lakeview High School in 1920, the same class as Connie Robertson. Snyder and Reynolds, a close friend of Daly's and a Fund trustee, were confident that young Howard would be among the first to get the Daly scholarship, but when the awarding of scholarships was held up because of the disputed will, they personally helped finance his pharmacy studies at Oregon Agricultural College.

While Howard was at school, Snyder bought out Reynolds, who focused on his role as a director at the Bank of Lakeview. Howard completed the two-year

---

*Daly began practice as a doctor in the early years of professionalization when doctors, lawyers, then pharmacists were first licensed. As part of that professionalization and to protect against conflict of interest, prescribing medicine was separated from dispensing and selling medicine.

pharmacy course and shortly after he returned, Snyder sold him a quarter interest in the store. The year was 1924, and the sign now read Snyder and Howard.

Clifton Howard became the sole owner in 1936, when Snyder left to sell insurance and serve in the state legislature. Clifton would be the first of four generations of pharmacists to work at Howard's Drug Store. Clifton's son, James, completed a four-year pharmacy degree at Oregon State College in 1950 and then returned to Lakeview to work with his father. James's son, Jeff Howard, graduated from Lakeview High School in 1976 in the same class as John Shine. Jeff received the Daly scholarship and went to Southern Oregon State College (now Southern Oregon University). As a prepharmacy student, he had lots of science classes and, as a member of the college swim team, he also had practices and meets. His grades suffered, and in his second year, he lost the Daly scholarship when his grades fell below the required GPA. While it was a setback for Jeff, it was an important indication of the integrity of the community entrusted with administering the scholarship. The year Jeff lost the scholarship, the chair of the Daly trustees was his mother, Dorothy Howard, the first woman to serve as chair.

Jeff persisted, and after three more years at Southern Oregon, he transferred to OSU. He married Melinda Gray, a 1979 LHS graduate and Daly Fund recipient who also transferred to OSU. While both were in pharmacy school there, they had the first of three sons, all of whom would receive the Daly scholarship. Two would become pharmacists and work with their parents. Only half-jokingly, Jeff told

Melinda and Jeff Howard with young Jacob Howard at their 1984 OSU graduation. (Courtesy of the Howard family)

me that Melinda, who received the Snyder scholarship for her fifth year at OSU, got him through pharmacy school. They graduated together in June of 1984 and returned to Lakeview to work with Jeff's dad in the drugstore. The sign now reads Howard's Drugs. So far, it's four generations of pharmacists and counting.

Jeff Howard and John Shine were among the 105 Lakeview High School graduates in 1976. During the 1970s, the graduating classes were especially large because of the boom in timber and lumber processing and also because of the students who came by bus from Bly in neighboring Klamath County. Bly, an unincorporated community just across the county line, was the home of a Weyerhaeuser lumber mill that employed about 240 people in 1979, more than half the town's total population.* After the Bly High School was condemned in the late 1960s, the students were given the choice of attending either Lakeview High School, about forty miles to the southeast, or Bonanza High School, about thirty-five miles to the southwest. Many chose Lakeview because of greater academic and sports opportunities. Those who went to Lakeview had bus rides of an hour each way. If they played sports, they had to take the smaller activity bus home later in the afternoon or well into the night. In winter, they would have to wait for the wrestlers to finish practice, then boys basketball, then finally girls basketball; there just wasn't much gym space. At times, they wouldn't return home until ten o'clock at night and would then have to be back for morning practice at six in the morning—and somehow find time for homework and chores. Some of the away games were so far away that the Bly kids didn't get home until after midnight.

The Bly kids went to Lakeview High School but were not eligible for the Daly or Collins McDonald scholarships. One of the former Bly students told me he never thought about it—that's just the way it was. Another said she felt bad that she didn't have the opportunity for the scholarship; another said that since she knew college wasn't a possibility, she didn't put in the extra effort to get As; another told me she was one of five girls from Bly to graduate in 1977, and that

---

*On the Lake County side of the county line near Bly was the only place on the US continent where death resulted from enemy action during World War II. On May 5, 1945, Reverend Archie Mitchell and his pregnant wife, Elsie, and five of his Sunday School students were on a picnic when a Japanese balloon bomb was accidentally detonated; only Reverend Mitchell survived. During the course of the War, more than 9,300 of these balloons flew along the easterly wind current. The balloon that found its way to Bly was the only one to result in casualties.

all five went to college, and three have master's degrees. It does seem that many did go on to college even though they were not eligible for the scholarships; they, too, were impacted by the college-going culture in Lakeview.

The last good year for Oregon's lumber industry was 1979, when 78,500 worked in Oregon's mills, more than a third of all of the state's manufacturing jobs. Oregon's economy tumbled; unemployment grew to 11.4 percent, one of the highest rates in the nation and the greatest in Oregon since records had been kept.[4] Most of the employment in Bly was lost, and in 1981, the Bly mill closed. A few years later, in 1984, only five Bly kids took the bus to Lakeview. After they graduated, the few kids remaining in Bly went to Bonanza High School in Klamath County. In just a decade, the Oregon timber industry went from boom to bust.

In the mid to late 1930s and into the '40s, Lake County lumber mills attracted migrant workers from the South and Dust Bowl regions. Jim Creel was among them. He grew up in logging camps in the pine forests of southeastern Oklahoma; in 1940, he hitched a ride to Lakeview with the Cossey family. Jim was sixteen and had $6.36 in his pocket. He went to work rigging with the McDonald Logging Company, where he was recognized as a particularly good worker, someone who knew his way around the woods. In describing those days working in the woods, Jim said, "It was a real thrill to me to see all of the timber. When we'd drive through the woods in the morning, we'd say loggers could never, ever harvest all of these trees. There seemed to be so much of it. Yet, since I've been here, they sure did harvest it all."[5]

Reportedly, Jim was the first man in Lake County to use a chainsaw and, in the early 1960s while still working in the woods, he started Jim's Saw Shop.[6] I met Jim's son, Craig, in Corvallis, where he worked for the US Forest Service Pacific Northwest Research Station, located on the OSU campus. Craig, a 1975 Lakeview High School graduate, told me that when he was about sixteen, he worked with his dad in the woods bucking, cutting limbs after the trees were cut. He remembers a particularly hot summer day when a Forest Service inspector came to the site. The inspector had a nice clean uniform and gave everyone drinks from a cooler in the back of his truck. This seemed like a better way to work in the woods, so Craig asked him how he got that job. The inspector told Craig that he had a forestry degree at OSU. That interaction gave Craig a clear goal to work toward. Though he did not get a scholarship, Craig was able to pay

for his own college costs through summer jobs with the Forest Service and working with his parents' Christmas tree business.* Like Jeff Howard, he started at
Southern Oregon State College and then transferred to OSU after a year. He
had a hard time at the larger school so went back to Southern Oregon College
for another year, then returned to OSU, where he completed his forestry degree
in 1983.

When Craig graduated and looked for work, Oregon was in the midst of its
worst economic downturn since the Great Depression. He worked at firefight-
ing and his family's Christmas tree business while searching for a job. He did get
a one-month job with the State Forestry Department, which turned into a permanent position. After a couple of years, he went to work at the Pacific Northwest
Research Station, where he was part of a group that did long-term research on
forest ecosystems, assessing impacts on water, geology, and climate. While his
dad imagined there were more trees than could ever be harvested and was surprised to see most of them cut down, his son would spend most of his career
adding to our understanding of trees and their role in nature.

While Craig worked in the woods during high school, all three of his sisters
worked at King's Café, Lakeview's only Chinese restaurant. The owner, King
Lee, came to America from China in 1948 with her husband, Bing, and a not-
yet-born baby daughter. With the Civil War in China between the Communists
and Nationalists, they decided to stay and somehow found their way to Lakeview,
where they opened King's Café in 1951. King Lee and her restaurant became
a Lakeview institution. Lots of Lakeview's high school and college students
worked there and were known as King's girls. Bing died in 1966, but King continued to cook and run the restaurant until her death in 2003—more than fifty
years, seven days a week, open until at least two in the morning, often later.

Everyone from Lakeview seems to have a story about King Lee, and there
are common themes. She was loving, kind, and tough. She loved the girls and
women who worked in the restaurant; they were like family. She provided help
and financial assistance, enabling some of the girls to go to college. Several told
me that when they returned from college, they went to see her before going to
see their own families. And she wasn't afraid of drunken cowboys or loggers. She

---

*In about 1965, Jim Creel brought Christmas trees down to the San Francisco area and
sold them directly to customers on a street corner. He was surprised at how many he
sold, so he continued the seasonal business for years.

stayed open after the bars in town closed; when there were fights, or especially if someone "crossed the line" with a waitress, she would come out of the kitchen with a broom or sometimes a meat cleaver. Jim Clinton, who was in high school in the late 1950s, remembered the restaurant and its owner:

> King's Café was a gathering place for Saturday night partiers, especially after the bars closed at 2:00. I remember frequent cases where guys would do stupid stuff just to get her agitated. In a one-cop town, it sometimes fell to her to get drunk fighters out of her front door and onto the sidewalk. We all used to laugh at these Monday morning stories in school and wonder how she did it. She certainly wasn't afraid of big ranchers in cowboy hats.

King's daughter, Barbara, told me the story of a sheepherder, fresh off the boat from Ireland, who had been out with a band of sheep for months by himself. When he returned to Lakeview, he went to King's Café and straight to the bar for drinks and then to the restaurant where he tried to order his meal. None of the waitresses could understand his thick Irish brogue. In frustration, he threw his hands up and said, "Get me Mama King." She came out of the kitchen and, although her English wasn't that good, she understood his order perfectly and couldn't understand why the waitresses had trouble.

Barbara grew up and went to school in Lakeview. She was the only student in her class and the entire school who was not white. Working at the Conn and Lynch Law Office one summer during high school, she remembers when the office received a letter asking about the number of minority students who had received the Daly scholarship. Ted Conn and Jim Lynch both read the letter and then looked up and saw Barbara in a new light. Barbara was a very good student and, as far as I can tell, she was the first nonwhite person to receive the Daly scholarship. Barbara graduated in 1966 and went to OSU, where she majored in business education. After graduating, she received the Snyder scholarship and started law school but realized it wasn't for her, so she began a successful career teaching in Oregon and Hawaii.

They all came from somewhere else: John Shine from Ireland, the Kovacsy family from Hungary, and King Lee from China. On July 5, 1956, they were all in the same room in the Lake County Courthouse, where a photograph was taken of them and others who received US citizenship that day in Lakeview.

1956 Citizenship Ceremony (King Lee, seated, first on left; Arpad Kovacsy with his mother and father, front row on the right; and John Shine Sr., back row, second from the right. (Courtesy of the Lake County Museum)

CHAPTER 7

FROM TIMBER TO TECH
1980s–1990s

*Their parents worked in the forest; they work in high tech.
Digging in the dirt. College tuition skyrockets, and so does
college debt. From a tiny school to work as a software
engineer. Small community seeks new, more balanced
relationship with nature. The Daly Fund receives
a multi-million-dollar gift.*

In the early 1980s, Liz VanLeeuwen showed up at the state legislature with her dishpan full of papers, reports, and newspaper clippings, and I began my OSU career as a young assistant professor in the College of Education. Those were hard times in Oregon. There was a severe recession, and the state was struggling to transition from a reliance on natural resources toward a more diversified economy. The 1980s were a turning point. It took most of the decade, but eventually Oregon's economy found its way to a blend of services, manufacturing, and high tech. But the new, more diversified economy was largely confined to the Portland metropolitan area. Lake County struggled as lumber mills closed and jobs were lost, yet Daly scholarships continued to be awarded every year to talented Lake County high school graduates, preparing them for a future that would increasingly have to be realized somewhere other than Lake County.

John Horne was the valedictorian of the 1980 Lakeview graduating class. Though he was not surprised to get the Daly scholarship, John still remembers the relief he felt knowing that he and his parents would not have to bear the full burden of college costs. In the fall, he was off to OSU, where he majored in civil engineering. He took a heavier course load than recommended and was crushed when his first term GPA was 2.46. Knowing that other Daly scholarship recipients had lost the scholarship because they could not maintain the required GPA,* John brought his grades up and kept them there.

The Lakeview community was proud of the Daly scholarship; it was something the entire community could rally around. It was as though the more than fifty-year-old scholarship had created a gravitational field that attracted other scholarships, contributions to existing scholarships, and a variety of in-school and out-of-school educational activities.

One example is the Eri Cup competition, a school-wide annual speech competition started by English teacher Roberta Bleakney in 1965. John is not the only former Lakeview student who told me about the Eri Cup; it seems to have had quite an impact. Built into the English curriculum, all Lakeview freshmen were required to give general informative speeches; sophomores, biographical talks; and juniors, persuasive speeches. The junior class finalists gave their speeches in front of the entire school, with community members and last year's finalists serving as judges.

As a junior, John was a finalist and first-runner up. He remembers speaking in front of the entire school but can't remember the topic of his speech. He does, however, remember the winning speech given by Lesa Lynch. Her speech was about the gestation and parturition of cattle with the aid of particularly graphic photos. Lesa and the other winners received the Eri Cup, donated by local businessman Wally Eri. Over the course of their high school years, most Lakeview students would give sixteen to eighteen speeches; those who were in the Future Farmers of America (FFA) might give as many as twenty-six. The Eri Cup built confidence in public speaking and also contributed to a comfort with academic competition. Much as the college literary society prepared Bernard Daly for public service, the Eri Cup competition helped prepare Lakeview students for future success at work and in the community.

As John was finishing his degree requirements at OSU, Oregon was still in recession, and civil engineering graduates had trouble finding jobs. Noticing that his roommates who majored in mechanical engineering all had job offers, John decided to stay on for another two years to complete an additional degree in mechanical engineering. It's an interesting choice. Most graduates who find

---

*John's GPA was actually above the required minimum for freshman, which was 2.2. The requirement for sophomores and juniors was 2.35; 2.5 for seniors. It may seem surprising that John remembered his first-term GPA (to the hundredth), but in my interviews with Daly scholarship recipients, I found many still remembered their college GPAs.

themselves in a poor job market are likely to look for any kind of job, even if they are underemployed relative to their degree preparation. John made a different choice, in large part because he had not assumed any debt to that point and had continuing support, having been awarded the Collins McDonald scholarship for one of the two additional years. Those two years were challenging. There were terms when he had both civil and mechanical engineering classes, but John persisted, graduating in 1986 with two degrees.

After graduating, he had many job offers; it seemed that everyone wanted the combination of civil and mechanical engineering. It's an unusual combination. John told me that in his career, he has only met one other engineer with both degrees. Partly because he wanted to stay in the Northwest, John took a job with Boeing, and with his employer's support, he immediately started on a master's degree in civil engineering at the University of Washington, where his advisor was Steve Kramer, a new faculty member who would become a world expert on earthquake engineering. John stayed on to earn his PhD and do research with Steve on how loose, sandy soil liquefies during an earthquake and, given the right circumstances, can knock over bridges and other structures.

After some time on the faculty at Clemson University, John returned to Portland, Oregon, where he is the assistant vice president and senior engineer for a large international consulting firm. With his civil and mechanical engineering background, John works on big projects that involve huge machines moving lots of earth while trying to account for natural forces that, over time, have the power to move mountains. He's worked on the building of the Bay Area Rapid Transit system, Alaska Way Viaduct tunnel in Seattle, and the California high-speed rail system, but it is his current project, the Mitchell Point Tunnel along the old Columbia River Highway, that he finds the most interesting and satisfying.

It's a project with some history. Mitchell Point is a basalt outcropping that rises a thousand feet above the nearby Columbia River. Shaped by the Missoula Floods that swept through the Columbia Gorge about thirteen thousand years ago, Mitchell Point has a steep, near-vertical pitch on its north face. In 1915, the historic Columbia River Highway included a 385-foot tunnel through the Mitchell Point basalt that featured five arched windows carved out of solid rock, offering spectacular views of the river below. The tunnel was destroyed, not by nature, but through the construction of Interstate 84 in the 1960s. The Oregon Department of Transportation is now rebuilding the Columbia River Highway, and John is leading the design for a new tunnel at Mitchell Point, complete with arched windows. It's not as big as other projects John has worked on, but it is an especially challenging one with great local and historic significance.[1]

The Lakeview mills were still busy in 1977 when Hobie Means and his family moved to Lakeview for Hobie to start a new job managing timber sales for the Forest Service. Hobie's first year in Lakeview was the last good year for Oregon's lumber industry. In 1978, about 240 million board feet of timber was harvested in Lake County; it would fall to about 50 million by the end of the 1990s.[2] With the decline in timber harvests came declines in employment and population. Lakeview's population reached its high of 3,260 in 1960; by the end of the 1990s, it was just under 2,500.

Hobie's daughter Shelley started eighth grade in Lakeview in the middle of the school year. It is hard to be the new kid in school, especially when you start in the middle of the year. She remembers two very good things that happened in her first few days at the new school. One was when she walked into the gym for her PE class; a Klamath Modoc Native American girl came over to her and said, "Hey, cousin, come on in." That was a particularly good thing for Shelley, who is Native American, a mixture of Ojibwe, Oglala Lakota, and some Finnish. (Her Finnish grandfather joked that she was an "unfinished Indian.") Having gone to school in several small rural communities, Shelley was used to being one of the few students of color, but it was good to know she was not the only one who looked different. Shelley was attuned to "otherness" and remembered how she was struck by the many Irish families in Lakeview. She loved learning about their families and history. Looking back on her time in Lakeview, she said, "there were the Irish and the rest of us."

The second good thing was that she met Linda Williams, a student in her class who volunteered to show Shelley around the school. Linda and Shelley became best friends, and more than forty years later, they still are. The youngest of three girls, Linda was born and raised in Lakeview. Though neither her mom or dad had gone to college, all three of their daughters received scholarships and went on to college. Linda was always the best student in her classes. When she was in the second or third grade, someone told her she would be the high school valedictorian. Linda was not sure what that meant, but that is exactly what happened. Shelley and Linda both became aware of the Daly Fund through their older sisters. Shelley's older sister was a high school sophomore when the family

Shelley Means and Linda Williams, friends then and now.

moved to Lakeview, so she was not eligible for the scholarship. Linda's two older sisters were eligible, and both received scholarships. Linda and Shelley did well all through school and were confident that they would receive the scholarship— and they did.

Linda, who always did well in math and science, went to OSU to study engineering, while Shelley followed her older sister to the University of Oregon and started off in international studies. OSU was somewhat of a shock for Linda. Her first term was not bad, but winter term was a lot harder. She was struggling with challenging classes and the adjustment of being away from Lakeview when she got 45 percent on a chemistry exam and was so devastated, she stopped going to class. Several weeks later, a student from the class recognized her and asked why she had not been to class. When Linda told him about her exam score, he said that her score may have been one of the highest and, since the instructor graded on a curve, it was probably an A or a B. Linda was shocked; she had never heard of grading on a curve, and it was too late in the term to go back to class. She dropped the class and signed up to take it again the next term. Halfway through that next term, the last of the year, Linda realized that she would finish the year two credits short of a year's full load, one of the Daly scholarship requirements.

Nervously, she went to see Franz Haun, the OSU advisor for Daly scholarship students and also OSU Director of New Student Programs.* Franz listened to her tale of woe and told her to come back next week so he would have time to think about it. When she returned, Franz sent her to meet with an anthropology instructor who gave her a stack of anthropology books and said, "Come back during finals week, and I'll quiz you on the material." When finals week came, she had not made it through all the books, but she did meet with the instructor and was successful in responding to the questions. It was a close call, but from then on, Linda maintained a full load, and then some, for the rest of her time at OSU.

Like many other Daly recipients, Linda worked during the summers fighting fires for the Bureau of Land Management. One of the reasons she liked the work was that Shelley was a dispatcher, and they saw and talked with each other most days. Working during the summers is what made it possible for Linda, Shelley, John, and many other Daly students to pay for college costs beyond those that were covered by the scholarship. The scholarship then, as it does now, covered about a third of the costs for tuition, fees, room, and board. When first awarded in the 1920s, the scholarship covered everything, including laundry and trips home during the year. But beginning in the 1930s, when the Fund's interest earnings plummeted and more students wanted to go to college, the scholarship amount was reduced at the same time tuition was going up. The Daly trustees eventually settled on scholarship awards that covered a third of estimated total costs. Over time, it has proved to be the right amount, just enough for students to make up the difference through summer work, part-time work during the school year, and careful management of expenses.

While Linda was well on her way to becoming an engineer, Shelley was not sure about her college major. She started in international studies because she liked different cultures and languages, but she became discouraged and was not sure what to study. Well aware of the scholarship requirement to maintain a full load and graduate in four years, Shelley chose journalism because most of the

---

*Franz Haun served as the Daly student advisor from 1967 until his retirement in 1997. At the time, each of Oregon's universities had a Daly Student Advisor; some, like Haun, were actively involved with the students, while others were more transactional. Several scholarship recipients told me that the Eastern Oregon University Daly advisor would invite all of the Daly students to his home for dinner at the beginning of each academic year.

credits she had already taken would count toward that major, enabling her to finish in four years. Shelley's push to pick a major that would allow her to finish in four years and stay in compliance with the scholarship requirement contrasts with the experience of many college students who switch from one major to another, hoping to find the right fit but ending up taking six years or more to complete their degrees.

As it turned out, journalism was a good major for Shelley, who liked to write and tell stories. After graduating in 1986, she moved to Seattle and found work with a young company that had just gone public that year—Microsoft. Shelley edited materials that would be translated into different languages. The corporate environment was not a good fit for Shelley, however, so she left after about a year. Had she stayed longer, she would have easily become a millionaire, but in retrospect, she is not at all sorry that her interests took her elsewhere. Those interests led her toward service to Native American communities, first for the City of Seattle, where she worked as a tribal liaison facilitating conversations between the tribes and the city on water rights and cultural resources. Those were conversations that could be traced all the way back to the 1854 Medicine Creek and 1855 Point Elliott Treaties between the United States and the tribes that occupied the lands around the Puget Sound. Like most US treaties with Native Americans, these enabled the "purchase" of tribal lands for pennies on the dollar, but unlike many other treaties, they also guaranteed the tribes' rights to hunt and fish in their usual grounds. It is those guaranteed rights that have been at issue for all these years.[3]

In most ways, the job as tribal liaison was suitable, but Shelley was uncomfortable being seen as only representing the city in those conversations, so she left. From that point on, she has worked for a variety of nonprofit organizations supporting the health and well-being of Native Americans. As a community organizer, she has worked in support of sacred site protection, health equity, environmental justice, and philanthropy for Native American causes. Shelley may have had difficulty finding her college major, but her life's work had no trouble finding her.

Though Linda started and finished in engineering, it was seven years before she graduated in 1989. It took somewhat longer than usual because Linda took many classes that did not count toward her industrial engineering degree, including a minor in Spanish, two full terms in Mexico, and two six-month internships, one at Freightliner and one at Intel. After graduation, Linda went to work for

Intel in Washington County, just west of Portland, where Intel was establishing its largest presence outside of its California headquarters. It was a remarkable time to be at Intel. Linda was part of the growth of the personal computer and the development of wireless technology. She remembers helping to develop an Intel PC-based video conferencing system in the early 1990s. While they were developing algorithms that capture and compress the view and audio streams, her team wondered, "Would anyone really want to see the person they were talking with?" They would, just not quite then; it would be twenty-five years before Skype, WhatsApp, FaceTime, and Zoom made video calls commonplace.

Linda Williams representing Intel in Japan.

During Linda's twenty-eight-year career, Intel grew to become Oregon's largest employer and the epicenter of what is now known as the Silicon Forest, a nod to California's Silicon Valley. The roots of Oregon's Silicon Forest can be traced back to Oregon's actual forests and the Forest Service Radio Lab's pioneering development of low-power, lightweight radios for communications with rangers and firefighters. Among those who worked with the Forest Service Lab were Douglas Strain and Howard Vollum. Strain went on to cofound Electro Scientific Industries, and Vollum was a cofounder of Tektronix. Those two pioneering Oregon tech companies, along with plentiful water and proximity to California's Silicon Valley, were important in attracting Intel and other tech companies. Roughly the same number of jobs that disappeared from Oregon's forests and mills in the 1980s appeared in the Silicon Forest of Washington County in the '90s as Intel and other companies invested billions of dollars in semiconductor facilities.[4]

After early retirement, Linda stayed busy, coaching women in high tech companies who were aiming for higher-level positions and volunteering at Adelante Mujeres, a nonprofit organization that provides opportunities to low-income Latina women and their families. She also has started an environmentally friendly goat field-clearing business. Here's Linda's description of her journey from Lake County to the Silicon Forest:

> I'm the first person on either side of my family to graduate from college. I owe it to the magic combination of great supportive parents, amazing, encouraging teachers at LHS, and the ability to pay for it with my parents help, Daly Fund, and fighting fires for the BLM in the summer. I'm 52 and recently retired from an amazing career at Intel Corp. I've been able to travel the world, work with amazingly smart humans and be a part of world-altering technical innovations. Now I have lots of time to give back to causes I care about. I am truly blessed and grateful for getting out of Lake County with a strong start—thanks, Dr. Daly, wherever you are!

Linda, Shelley, and John are among the many scholarship recipients who never returned to live in Lakeview after graduating from college. Their degrees prepared them for life and work someplace other than Lake County. Education and mobility are highly correlated, so it is not surprising that most of the students who received the scholarship left and never returned. One who did return was Ann (Rago) Crumrine, a 1991 Lakeview High School graduate. Since Ann planned to attend Linfield College, a small private college, she received the Collins McDonald Scholarship rather than the Daly scholarship, which could only be used at an Oregon public college. The Collins McDonald Scholarship operated under the same rules as the Bernard Daly Scholarship, and both funds were administered by Jim Lynch, the longtime Daly Fund administrator. Ann told me that she, as so many others I interviewed, remembers going to Jim Lynch's law office to turn in a copy of her grades and pick up the check for each term. It was a simple and effective form of accountability. All of the scholarship recipients knew that the local scholarship administrators kept track of their grades, and they also knew that the checks would stop if their grades fell below the required GPA or if they did not maintain a full load. They had a strong incentive to do well and finish in four years.

At Linfield, Ann majored in finance, minored in economics, and played on the college volleyball team. She was busy during the year and also in the summers, when she fought fires back in Lake County. The summer of 1992 was particularly memorable; there were so many fires that Ann worked every single day, including Saturdays and Sundays, from July Fourth until she reported to Linfield for volleyball practice at the end of the summer. With hazard and overtime pay, she made about $10,000 that summer. Not every summer was like that; the next was especially rainy with few fires so she only made about $5,000. Ann needed to make as much money as possible because Linfield's tuition was quite a bit more than at the state-supported colleges on which the scholarship award was based. In 1991, Linfield's tuition and fees were a bit more than $13,000, about five times the tuition at OSU. Even with the scholarship, fighting fires in the summer, and support from her parents, she still needed to borrow $8,000. Ann remembered that many of her Linfield classmates had student loans much greater than hers. She was right—the nineties were a time of rapidly rising tuition and student debt.

While Ann was in college, two important changes led to greater student borrowing. The first was that the cost of going to college increased much faster than inflation. The second was that the 1992 Reauthorization of the Higher Education Act increased loan limits, expanded eligibility for need-based aid, and introduced unsubsidized Stafford loans for students regardless of their financial need. The resulting increase in student loans was immediate and dramatic. In the first year after the change, total student loan volume increased by

35 percent; by the end of the 1990s, it would increase more than 100 percent.[5] Increases in tuition were driven in part by declining state support for colleges. When the Daly scholarship was first awarded in the early 1920s, states provided most of the funding for state-supported colleges. When I started at OSU in 1981, the state of Oregon provided about 40 percent of OSU's total revenue; when I retired in 2016, the state's contribution was less than 10 percent. States had become minority investors in their own colleges, and skyrocketing student tuition would make up the difference. While it had taken more than a hundred years for OSU's annual tuition to reach $1,000 in the early 1980s, in the mid-1990s, just fifteen years later, it would be over $10,000.

Busy as Ann was, she still managed to graduate in just three and a half years. After graduation, she returned to Lakeview and worked in a variety of jobs—at the local bank, an insurance agency, the Coca-Cola dealership, and then finally, in 1999, she began working for the Lake County Finance Department, eventually becoming the county treasurer. As county treasurer, Ann is in an especially good position to consider the economic impact of the Daly scholarship on the county. While the scholarship's impact on the recipients is clear, the impact on Lake County is more nuanced. When I first met with Jim Lynch to discuss the scholarship, he told me that within the community, the scholarship has been criticized because it has educated the best and the brightest, leading to them moving away from the county. When I asked Ann about this brain drain, she said, "I'm a strong proponent of education as an economic driver, whether it stays in the community or not. People move away but stay connected and supportive of Lake County." Yes, there is a connection; some, like John Shine, do return after they retire, and many return for class reunions and visits. It is an issue that strikes close to home for Ann as her son and daughter both received scholarships and are likely to live and work somewhere far from Lake County.

Luke Dary's work took him about as far away from Lake County as is possible. I met Luke in Raleigh, North Carolina, at the headquarters of Red Hat, a world leader in enterprise open-source software, where Luke is a principal web development engineer and somewhat of a social media star in the world of web development. Where he lives and what he does are both a long way from Adel, where he grew up and attended the same tiny school that the Shine kids attended twenty years earlier. The Adel school had two teachers, a talented husband-and-wife teaching staff. Ty Tuchscherer taught grades six to eight, while his wife, Pam, taught grades three to five in the older building next door.

Luke and his classmates (all of them) were on the Adel math team that won the regional MATHCOUNTS competition by edging out the much bigger Klamath Falls junior high team. Luke did especially well in math, completing calculus as a junior in high school and graduating near the top of his class in 1998.

Luke's high school years were a challenging time for the Lakeview community. Conflict between the timber industry and environmentalists had come to a head as more stringent environmental regulations led to the closing of four of the five Lakeview mills. Only one working mill, the Fremont Sawmill, remained, and it, too, was in danger of closing. That mill and much of the Lakeview economy depended on federal timber sales from the five-hundred-thousand-acre Lakeview Federal Sustained Yield Unit of the Fremont Forest. Future sales were in question as environmental concerns threatened a new agreement with the Forest Service. Facing grim prospects, the community came together to form the Lakeview Stewardship Group with a vision for a sustainable, healthy forest. The new group hosted meetings with environmentalists, scientists, Forest Service officials, and representatives of the remaining mill. It took time, tensions were high, and not everyone wanted to work together, but the group persisted, and the result was a new agreement permitting sustainable, small-diameter logging. Central to the agreement was a commitment to ongoing monitoring of forest health by Lakeview science teacher Clair Thomas and a group of his talented students, including Luke.[6]

With the support of the Daly scholarship, Luke went to OSU, where he majored in business with a management information systems emphasis. He worked as much as thirty hours a week during the school year, providing tech support for the campus residence halls. It may seem odd that a kid who went to a small rural school was hooking up computers and solving tech problems for kids from the wealthier areas of Portland, but that's what Luke did, and it's not far from what he does now. After four years at OSU, Luke had not quite finished his degree requirements, and, as John and Linda, he did something different. Luke took a year off to go back to Lakeview and work with Clair Thomas on the Chewaucan Biophysical Monitoring team that was gathering data on how forest health was responding to timber harvest strategies. For each one-tenth-acre plot, Clair and his crew of high school and college students collected data on every tree over ten centimeters in diameter as well as data on water, macro invertebrates (insects), understory thinning, and soil compaction—lots of data. And that's where Luke came in. Clair and his team tried to use off-the-shelf database

Luke Dary at Red Hat Headquarters.

software to catalog the extensive data, but it was not working well. So, in 2002, during his year away from OSU, Luke created a database program that enabled efficient data entry and queries—all of which informed forest management practices. Almost a decade later, high school and college kids are still monitoring the forests, and Luke, now a Red Hat software engineer, has been spending some of some of his spare time to update the forest monitoring database to a more modern web paradigm.

The success of Lakeview Stewardship Group led to the formation of the Lake County Resource Initiative with a much broader mission of seeking a more healthy relationship between the people of Lake County and their natural environment, all of it—land, water, air, and plant and animal life. It's an ambitious mission. After a century of extracting resources from the land with little regard for the consequences, Lake County took a turn toward a more sustainable future.

Jess and Alta Roberts made their fortune from the forests and lands of Lake County, along with a lot of hard work. Jess was an "Okie" who came to Oregon as a boy with his family in the 1920s. As a young man, Jess and his wife, Alta, traveled with timber camps through Lake County forests; Jess worked with the loggers, while Alta cooked in a cook shack that was hauled by horses from camp to camp. In time, Jess transitioned from logging to building logging roads and then to ranching. Their ranch operation grew and prospered. Like Daly, they had no direct heirs, and as part of their estate, they left more than $2 million to be added to the Daly Fund, investing much of their fortune in the futures of Lake County youth.

In Lakeview High School, just next to a bronze bust of Bernard Daly, there are busts of Jess and Alta Roberts with an inscription that includes their personal philosophy: "There is not better use of life than to use it for something that will outlast it."

CHAPTER 8

A NEW MILLENNIUM
2000s

*An artist and animal trapper. Managing the money behind
college sports. An expat cyclist living in Italy teaching children
in China. My first of many visits to Lakeview. I ride my bike
to Lakeview to attend the trustee meeting, and keep going.
Max climbs and codes. Is there something in the water?*

Those who graduated and entered into adulthood in the early 2000s are called millennials. There are now more of them living than those in their parents' generation, the baby boomers. In comparison with the boomer generation, they are better educated, more diverse, and less likely to marry and have families. They have also been described as technically savvy, open to change, free-thinking, and team players.[1] All that may be so, but when I think about three young women who received the Daly scholarship in 2001, the word that comes to my mind is brave. Three brave young women from Lakeview found their way to very different places and very different types of work: one to Brooklyn, where she is an artist and animal trapper; one who became the chief financial officer for OSU Athletics in Corvallis; and one who lives in northern Italy, where she is a writer, leads bike tours, and teaches English to children in China.

The Lake County landscape stays with all who experience it. It's high desert country, with elevations greater than a mile and mountain peaks approaching ten thousand feet. It's a cold desert, with sage, grassland, and majestic pine forests growing on the tops of mountain ranges that overlook a landscape of ancient lakes. Sarah Hollars (LHS 2001) was captivated by the Lake County landscape and took it with her when she left for college, then to art studies in Europe and on to Brooklyn, where she is an artist and animal trapper.

When she was young, Sarah learned to hunt, tromping through the fields with her dad in search of ducks, deer, and antelope. She was active in 4-H, raising and showing pigs and rabbits at the county fair. By the time she was in middle school, Sarah was fully immersed in art and well aware of the Daly scholarship. Her English teacher, Lisa Shullanberger, remembers that Sarah was all in when involved in any type of art. In particular, Lisa remembered the time Sarah cut her hair to look like the character she was portraying in a school play and memorized every single line. In 2001, when Sarah graduated from high school, she was one of twenty-three Daly scholarship recipients. Sarah wanted to go to an art school but, in retrospect, was glad she listened to her mom and went to the University of Washington. As has been done for many other Daly recipients, when Sarah decided to attend the University of Washington rather than an Oregon public university, her scholarship was switched to the Collins McDonald, which permitted enrollment at out-of-state institutions. Trying to be practical, she majored in graphic design, but after exchange programs in London and Rome, where she experienced artistic masterpieces up close, she left graphic design behind and set off on the path of an artist.

After completing her degree at the University of Washington, she was on to the University of Oregon for a degree in fine arts, and then, with the support of several scholarships,* to New York City for a master's degree at Hunter College. Armed with three art degrees, Sarah was well into an artist's life–painting, hustling to get into exhibits, and teaching a few art classes at Hunter College. If you do a web search for Sarah Hollars, you will see several of her paintings. They're large, with layers of color depicting vast landscapes punctuated with small figures and animals. Much of her work draws on her roots in Lake County. She explains: "In Lake County you can see so far and the animals are indicators of depth, space, and location." She invokes a spirituality that comes from the landscape, noting that "It's about the landscape and the feelings that come from being there. There's something about how humans experience landscapes that transcends cultures and location."[2]

Just as she tired of negotiating the challenging marketplace for art, Sarah found her way into a very different type of work. It started with a neighbor who

---

*Through a combination of scholarships and part-time and summer work, Sarah completed three art degrees without assuming debt. One of those scholarships was an award from the Aaron Osborne Memorial Fund. Aaron Osborne was also a 1965 Daly scholarship recipient, and, he too, followed an artistic pursuit. At first, Aaron was a pre-med student at the University of Oregon, but when he took a dance class to satisfy the physical education requirement, he found his life's work. He transferred to the Julliard in New York City, where he studied dance and went on to a distinguished career as a dancer and teacher.

"Just Flesh And Bones," painting Sarah Hollars, oil on
canvas, 98″ x 78″ (2012).

complained that a stray cat she fed was pregnant again. The neighbor wondered,
was there something that could be done? Sarah wanted to help, so she did some
research and learned about the Trap-Neuter-Return (TNR) program intended
to slow the growing population of stray cats. Sarah used a humane catch-and-
release trap to catch the neighbor's cat and then each of the kittens. That experience led to what she described as an addiction to trapping and a new job as the
community cats coordinator for the Animal Care Centers of New York City. It's
a big and challenging job as there are an estimated five hundred thousand "community cats" in New York City.* An important part of her job is teaching people
how to live trap, which is very much like hunting, something most New York
City residents have never experienced. She is still very involved in art, but she

---

*Through the Feral Cat Initiative, New York City recognizes community cats as com-
panion animals, not wildlife. As such, they are protected from the same anticruelty
statutes that protect pets. New York City's local laws endorse TNR and include vaccination for rabies and identification (ear tipping) in its definition of TNR. Bideawee,
"Community Cats & The Law," n.d.

now enjoys a much more personal relationship with her painting. When I asked Sarah to describe the impact of the Daly scholarship, she said, "It changed my life; it made me so much braver."

Jacque (Johnson) Bruns, who graduated with Sarah in 2001, also found her way to a big and challenging job as the chief financial officer (CFO) for OSU Athletics, an $80 million-dollar-a-year enterprise. With television contracts, endorsement and licensing deals, and generous donors, athletic programs at OSU and other major universities are making more money than ever before. The problem is they are also spending more money than ever, competing with each other for new facilities and highly paid coaches. In the best of times, balancing the athletic budget is like trying to herd cats; during the pandemic that began in 2020, it was a disaster. With shortened seasons and fans prohibited from attending games, OSU and athletic programs across the country lost revenue while facing unforeseen costs related to the virus. Jacque and others at OSU Athletics were forced to make tough choices and painful budget cuts.

Athletics at OSU and other colleges is a male-dominated field, and when Jacque was appointed as the CFO for OSU Athletics in 2017, she became the first woman to serve in that position at OSU as well as in the entire PAC-12 Conference. When I asked Jacque what it is like for her to be in that position, she said, "I see it as an opportunity for myself, my coworkers, and other women in the athletics department to all learn and grow. As a woman in this situation, I think the important thing to remember is that I do have an important voice."

Jacque's journey to become one of the few women CFOs in college athletics began in the small community of Lakeview, where she was born and raised, living in the same house until she left for college. Both of her parents were teachers, and Jacque was an especially hardworking and good student, active in sports and student government, both of which were good preparation for her future job. After high school, she first went to the University of Hawaii with the help of the Collins McDonald scholarship, but after a year, she transferred to OSU (and to the Daly scholarship) and completed a degree in business administration with an option in accounting and a minor in athletic administration. While she was a student, Jacque worked part-time in the athletics office preparing travel reimbursement forms. Every summer, she fought fires back in Lake County. She was busy, but even with the transfer from Hawaii, she graduated in four years. When I asked about it, she told me that "part of the beauty of the scholarship is that it keeps you on track."

After graduation from OSU, Jacque continued to work in the athletics business office. She also coached high school volleyball and somehow found the time to complete a master's degree in business administration at OSU. Starting from the bottom, she worked her way to the top of the business of sports at OSU.

Sylva Florence, who graduated with Sarah and Jacque, might have the biggest and most challenging job of the three—she has to keep up with herself, and that's not easy to do as she throws herself into one adventure after another. As with Sarah and Jacque, it all started in Lakeview, where Sylva grew up, went to school, and fell in love with singing and writing. She followed the music to Southern Oregon University, where she started as an opera major but soon switched to journalism. Toward the end of her first year of college, she decided at the last minute to participate in the National Student Exchange. Since it was late in the process, she had to choose among the few remaining colleges with journalism programs. That's how Sylva found her way to Indiana University of Pennsylvania (IUP). After a year there, Sylva transferred to James Madison University in Virginia, where she continued her journalism studies and, as she did at IUP, served as an editor of the student newspaper. Sylva graduated in 2005; three colleges and she still finished in four years through a combination of hard work and the push of the scholarship requirement.

Not wanting to stay on the East Coast, Sylva found a job fighting fires in Colorado. While living in Colorado, she did a lot of different things, often several at a time: back-country snow ranger, wilderness ranger, Starbucks barista, bartender, airport luggage handler, van driver, nanny, and freelance writer. On top of all that, beginning in 2009, she went to Italy each year to lead bike tours for American and Canadian cyclists. As she wrote in one of her blog entries, "I was logging 60-70 hours a week at two jobs to save up for whatever was next."[3]

What came next was a solo self-supported cycling trip across the southern United States. On her own for a little more than four months, Sylva rode her bike over four thousand miles, from Berkeley, California, to St. Augustine, Florida. Riding across the South in 2017, the year after the polarizing election of 2016, must have been quite an experience. As she wrote, "Turns out, I undertook a rather timely experience. During the era of 'me too,' I traveled across the USA as a solo female. Simultaneously, I threaded through areas of our very divided country—like the South—that many Americans view as unfriendly and unwelcoming. However, I discovered a very different America: a kind, welcoming America, across the board."[4]

Sylva Florence on her 2017 cross-country bike trip.

After a close-up view of her own country, Sylva packed up and moved to Faenza, a smallish city in north central Italy, where she lives in a building that dates back to the 1300s. In Italy, Sylva is again juggling several different jobs: freelance editing and translation, writing a book about her cross-country bike trip, and teaching English online to children in China. She may be far from home, but the feel of the Lake County landscape is with her. An entry from her blog:

> In Italy, very little actual wild lands remain. Even in the north where the jagged Dolomites challenge Italians to cultivate steep slopes, many still manage to do so. It's common to hike up avalanche paths and steep valleys for hours only to run into a rancher in a mud-splat-tered Fiat Panda tending to his sheep. As such, it's a challenge for an American like me, who grew up next to the wilderness, to find solitude. But when the trail winds on and off of this old dirt road, even though the road itself is evidence of human impact, the feeling of remoteness is achieved. The sounds of traffic have faded, and only on weekends

do hikers make it past the panoramic ridge. A distant dwelling might break up the forest, but it's mostly a big puzzle of mountains, clouds and sky.[5]

In 2010, I did not know anything about Sylva, Jacque, Sarah, or any Daly scholarship recipients other than Dan Dunham, who told me about Bernard Daly and the scholarship almost thirty years earlier. For some reason, the story of the scholarship stuck with me, and at one of the many OSU alumni gatherings I attended while serving as dean of OSU's College of Education, I met Sue (Ogle) Densmore. When Sue mentioned that she was from Lakeview, I asked about the scholarship and learned that Sue and both of her sisters had been recipients, and so were their parents, Jim and Dorothy Ogle. At the time, I was planning to step down as dean and return to a faculty position before retiring, and I was looking for a research project I could start and possibly work on in retirement. When Sue suggested I go to the annual breakfast her parents hosted at their ranch on Labor Day weekend, I jumped at the opportunity.

It was on that first visit to Lakeview in September of 2010 that I met Jim Lynch, the longtime secretary-treasurer for the Daly Fund. We met in the basement of his law office, surrounded by file cabinets, lawbooks, and a large framed photograph of Bernard Daly. In his understated and direct manner, Jim patiently answered my questions about the scholarship and its management over the years. It was a lot to absorb, but I left with a general understanding of how the scholarship worked and some sense of its impact. I also left with suggestions of others to visit in Lakeview and a list of all the recipients since the scholarship was first awarded in 1922. It was a spreadsheet with about two thousand names—just names with the year of graduation—and no addresses or contact information of any kind. I remember wondering how I could reach people for a survey or inter- views. Many would have passed away, and many of the living recipients would have moved away from Lake County. To further complicate matters, most of the women would have changed their names when they married.

I was intrigued and went back to Lakeview the very next month to meet with some of the people Jim Lynch had suggested. With each conversation I became more excited about the research possibilities. I learned about families with multiple generations of scholarship recipients from Bill Barry and Dorothy and Melinda Howard; about the local schools from Judy Graham, Sean Gallagher, Barb Simpson, and Sharon Faulkner; and more about the workings of the

Jim Lynch in the basement of his law office with photo of Bernard Daly (2010). (Author photo)

scholarship from Daly trustees Ann Tracy and Mike Sabin. After returning to Corvallis, I sent an email to the Daly scholarship students at OSU, inviting them for some pizza and conversation about the scholarship. About a half dozen came, mostly freshmen and sophomores, not far removed from high school. They were enthusiastic, hardworking students. I was particularly struck by the comments of Jonathan Boothe (LHS 2009), a sophomore majoring in biochemistry who laughed as he said: "The whole time I was in high school, they kept telling me about the Daly Fund. I didn't really know what the Daly Fund really was because my family hadn't been there that long. Then I started to figure out—wait, they give you money to go to school... this is a great idea." *

---

* Jonathan Boothe completed his degree in biochemistry at OSU in 2013. He now works at the US Geological Survey (USGS) in Denver, Colorado, analyzing water samples from around the country checking for pesticides and pharmaceuticals.

The next month, I drove to Eugene and spent a half day at the University of Oregon Archives, going through the contents of the Pearl Hall Collection. After reading the letters written between Bernard Daly and Pearl Hall, the press clippings she had saved, and her notes for a book about Daly, I was even more convinced that it was a project worth doing, and I wanted to do it. I just could not do it then as I was in my last few years as dean, and I had committed to a sabbatical research project that would take me to Tokyo and then Paris to work at the Organization for Economic Development and Cooperation (OECD). The project would have to wait.

About five years after that first visit to Lakeview, I was finally in a position to start on the project and was especially fortunate to connect with Jordan Hensley, a first-year public policy master's student interested in working with me. Together we began planning for a web-based survey of scholarship recipients, and in the spring of 2016, we made a trip to Lakeview. On that visit, we met with Jim Lynch's law partner, Dave Vandenberg (LHS 1981), who was taking over the position of secretary-treasurer for the Daly Fund. Dave, who was a Collins McDonald scholarship recipient, updated us on the scholarship, and we talked about our plans for the survey and my upcoming summer cross-country

Sam Stern with Jim Ogle in 2016.

bike trip. To celebrate my transition into retirement, I had planned to ride my bicycle cross-country, beginning on the Oregon Coast, riding first to Lakeview to attend the June trustee meeting, and then continuing to the East Coast.

It took me six days to ride from the town of Florence on the Oregon coast, up and over the beautiful McKenzie Pass, and then through Summer Lake, Silver Lake, and Paisley on the way to Lakeview. While riding, I thought about the Oregon State University and University of Oregon presidents who had traveled for three days to get to Lakeview for the annual trustee meeting in the early years of the scholarship. Over the years, that responsibility shifted from presidents to vice presidents and, more recently, to the administrators responsible for scholarships and financial aid. Jordan met me in Lakeview, and the two of us were among a handful of guests who attended the 2016 annual meeting with the trustees and representatives from each of Oregon's public colleges and Lake County high schools—about twenty-five attendees in total.

The half-day meeting began with the approval of the 2015 meeting minutes and the financial report detailing the balance of the Daly Fund, which at the time was about $5.5 million. After discussing student issues that had come up during the past year (i.e., requests for educational and medical leaves), there was a report on the total estimated cost of attendance at Oregon public colleges. According to the Oregon Higher Education Coordinating Commission, the cost was $24,192 that year. As in past years, the annual scholarship award would be one-third of the total estimated cost of attendance. Next came reports on other Lake County scholarships, including the relatively new Ousley Fund, first awarded in 2011. The Ousley scholarship was established in 2011 with an endowment of about $11 million through the estate of James Heryford Ousley,* who graduated in 1935, was a Daly recipient, and whose estate also made a generous gift to the Daly Fund. After reports on other county scholarships, each university representative reported on credits completed and grade point averages for Daly students attending their respective colleges.

Next came the heart of the meeting: the selection of the scholarship recipients. Each trustee received a list of all the applicants, ranked in order based

---

*After graduating from Lakeview High School in 1935, James Heryford Ousley went to the University of Oregon and then lived in the Los Angeles area, where he was a sales representative for an office equipment company. Much the same as Bernard Daly, he was a shrewd investor, and as he too never married, he left his entire estate to establish a scholarship for the youth of Lake and Klamath counties.

on each student's combined SAT scores and high school grade point average, but without names. Knowing the amount of committed funds for continuing scholarship students and the award amount per new student, the trustees were able to determine the number of scholarships that could be awarded that year; in other words, how far down the list they could go. Of the fifty-nine Lake County high school graduates who applied for the scholarship that year, twenty-five were awarded Daly scholarships. About the same number were awarded either Collins McDonald or Ousley scholarships, making it possible for almost all who wanted to go to college to receive scholarships.

The trustees also considered issues related to applicants and continuing students. What should be done when an applicant attends a portion of high school outside of the county or a continuing student fails to complete the required college credits because of an illness? I was impressed with the care and consideration given to each issue as they were discussed and then voted on. At the conclusion of the meeting, a final list of recipients was prepared, then posted that afternoon on the windows of the Lynch and Vandenberg law office and Howard's Drugs. As in past years, many would go out of their way to check the lists, looking for their names. That evening, at the dinner for trustees and guests, I got into a conversation with Noni Vandenberg, a math teacher at the high school and a cyclist. Noni told me about her weekend bike rides and also about the annual field trips she took with her eighth grade math students so they could learn about career opportunities for graduates with good math skills. We talked about the possibility of a visit to OSU sometime in the next spring.

On the next day, I continued on my cross-country bike trip, riding north on Route 395, one of Oregon's least-traveled roads. During the hundred-plus miles to Riley, I had lots of time to think about the trustee meeting as I saw only a few cars and a couple of buildings—not much that was manmade, but lots of natural beauty. Another day of riding, and I was in Burns, where I met Anne (Barry) Kness (LHS 1974), a recently retired physical education teacher who had been a gymnast during her time at OSU. Among other things, Anne told me about the responsibility she felt to live up to the expectation that came with the scholarship—she described it as a kind of personal accountability. A couple of days of riding later I was in Baker City, where I met Erin (Harlan) Taggart (LHS 2004) and her two sons. Erin went to Eastern Oregon University (EOU), fighting fires in the summer and graduating in four years with no debt. As I rode from Baker City into Idaho, toward Montana, I thought about something Erin said. When I asked about the impact on so many Lake County young women who received the scholarships, she spoke without hesitation, telling me that she and other women who received the scholarship simply have more choices. In Erin's case, her choice at the time was to be a stay-at-home mom, but she knew, if necessary, she could work to support her family.

In Missoula, I met Gary and Sidney (Harlan) Reynolds, both of whom graduated from Lakeview High School in 1962. They had known each other since they were eleven and had just celebrated their fiftieth wedding anniversary. Each has considerable history with the scholarship. Gary received the Daly scholarship, and so did his mother, Francis Burch (LHS 1930). His grandfather, Fred Reynolds, was Daly's close friend and longtime business partner, one of the executors of Daly's estate, and the first president of the Daly Fund trustees. Sidney's mother, Margaret Iverson, graduated from Silver Lake High School in 1940, one of only two graduates that year; both received the scholarship.*

The visits were great, giving me much to think about while riding toward the East Coast. There was lots of time for reflection as it turned out to be a three-month trip of more than forty-five hundred miles. Shortly after I returned to Corvallis by plane, Jordan and I launched our web survey. Thanks to the email addresses gathered from our Facebook page and the cooperation of both the Oregon State University and University of Oregon foundations, we received just over three hundred survey responses, about 20 percent of the estimated population of living recipients.** The survey results revealed much about the scholarship's educational and economic impact, but my experiences meeting people on the bike trip taught me that there was more to be learned from the recipients themselves. So I continued interviewing recipients in person and by phone; from that point on, whenever I traveled, I checked to see if there was a Daly Fund recipient near my destination.

---

*Just a couple of years after Margaret Iverson and her one classmate, Julia O'Keeffe, graduated, the small Silver Lake High School closed. For the next fifty years, from 1942 until the North Lake High School opened in 1992, students from that area took the long bus ride to the Paisley High School, about fifty miles south of Silver Lake.

**At the time of the survey, there were a total of 1,918 scholarship recipients since the scholarship was first awarded in 1922. We estimated that any recipient who had graduated before 1950 was likely to be deceased; therefore, the estimated living population of scholarship recipients was 1,471.

That is how I came to meet Max McKinnon (LHS 2007) at a San Jose coffee shop one morning before he went to work. I had gone to the Bay Area to visit my son, who worked at Apple, so was surprised to learn that Max also worked at Apple, where he developed an anomaly detection tool that still runs on the iPhone, Apple watch, iPad, and MacBook. On Max's website, this is how he describes what he does: "I build hardware and software tools. When I'm not doing that, I enjoy rock climbing, playing heavy metal guitar, and reading Chinese short stories." Once again I found myself wondering, how did Max get from Lakeview to the Bay Area, working at Apple, one of the most difficult places for anyone to get a job?

Max remembers first learning about the scholarship when he was in middle school, shortly after his family moved to Lakeview. It was in middle school where his science teacher, Ty Tuchscherer,* who previously taught Luke Dary in Adel, encouraged Max's interest in math and experimentation. In Ty's middle school math class, Max helped develop activities for calculator-controlled robots with sensors designed to go on rescue missions into collapsed buildings—exciting stuff. Max already had considerable interest in science as both of his parents had science backgrounds. After graduating and receiving the Daly scholarship, Max went to Oregon Institute of Technology (OIT), where he majored in electrical engineering because he wanted to understand how electric guitar pedals worked. He did learn more about electric guitar pedals and also completed two degrees, one in engineering and one in math, while working as a tutor and residence hall advisor. After graduating from OIT in four years, Max went on to graduate work in computer science at the University of Idaho and then jumped into the world of high tech, first at Maxim, then Apple, and now Google, where he is part of a team that is fighting misinformation through the development of an "About This Result" link for Google searches.

---

*Ty Tuchscherer was one of many extraordinary Lake County teachers. Ty and his wife, Pam, taught in Adel from 1990 to 1996, then in Bly for a year. Pam continued in Bly, while Ty moved to the Lakeview middle school, where he taught science and math until 2005, when he was awarded a fellowship as a NASA Einstein Fellow for his pioneering work in the use of 'calcbots' (calculator-controlled robots) for science and math education. As part of his NASA fellowship, Ty developed curricular materials for 'calcbots' that have been used in science and math classes throughout the country.

Max McKinnon at San Jose coffee shop in 2018.
(Author photo)

Max and Luke Dary are not the only ones from Lakeview who excelled in math. There seems to be a strong math tradition in Lakeview. When I finished my bike trip in the fall of 2016, I was stunned by the tragic news that Noni Vandenberg had been killed by a drunk driver while she was on a bike ride.* Wanting to follow up on my offer to Noni of arranging for an OSU field trip, I contacted Will Cahill, the Lake County School Superintendent, who put me in touch with Mark Louie, the teacher who took Noni's place. Together we started what has become an annual visit to OSU. The annual eighth grade advanced math field trip is

---

*Noni's Trail, a single-track mountain-bike trail that starts in Lakeview and goes through Bullard Canyon, was created in her memory. For more information on the trail, see https://www.mtbproject.com/trail/7049970/nonis-trail.

especially important because these students are in their first of four years of math, which will lead them all the way to calculus in their senior year. Only about 15 percent of America's high school students take calculus in high school, but over the past several years, about 25 percent of Lakeview High School graduates have taken calculus[6]. That's an especially high percentage for a small school—it's hard to offer calculus in a small school. First, you need a critical mass, enough students to offer the class every year. With average graduating classes of about sixty, Lakeview needs at least twelve students (20 percent) prepared to take calculus in their senior year for it to be viable. And they need a math teacher who is qualified to teach calculus and, more importantly, who knows how to relate the subject to kids. That's not all; it won't happen if you don't have kids who *want* to take calculus. Somehow Lakeview has created a culture that supports calculus. Luke Dary, Max McKinnon, and Jonathan Boothe (whom I met at the pizza gathering at OSU) all completed calculus in high school and went on to science and engineering careers. But it is not only the students going on to careers in science

Lakeview 8th grade advanced math OSU field trip (2019). Front row, L - R: Sam Stern, OSU; Zachary Turner; Mark Louie, math teacher; LeAnn Dillavou; Jaila Jackson; Kaydyn Kintzky second row - Orion Misner; Adriana Ishida; Levi Gruber; Karlee Vickerman; Audrey Rucker; third row - Shannon Smith, math teacher; fourth row - Trevor Owens; Wyatt Julian; Rebekah Patzke; Tyler McNeley; Annikah Tacchini; Karlee Vickerman; Bridget Shullanberger. (Courtesy of Lake County School District)

and engineering who take calculus; so did Jacque (Johnson) Bruns, who went on
to a career in athletic administration; Sarah Hollars, the artist and animal trapper; and many others, including the young woman math teacher Mark Louie told
me about during a recent field trip to OSU. She had taken his calculus class the
previous year and was one of the seventeen students who received that year's
Daly scholarship. After graduation, she went on to a community college cosme-
tology program. Will she use differential equations in hair styling? Probably not,
but the logic and reasoning she developed will come in handy, no matter what
she does.

Over the years, I've told friends stories about the scholarship recipients; after
hearing them, some have asked, "Is there something special in the Lake County
water?" There may be, but that's not what led to the extraordinary success of the
scholarship and its recipients. The scholarship was the catalyst that set a great
many things into motion: the creation of other scholarships, a community's support for education, excellent teaching, and, above all, motivated students. I think
about that each spring when I meet with the eighth grade math students who
come to OSU to learn about career possibilities. I wonder where they'll go and
what they'll do in their future. Based on what I've learned, it seems they can go
anywhere and do absolutely anything. While it may be hard to get to Lakeview, it
seems that Lakeview kids can go anywhere.

EPILOGUE

It is tempting to call Bernard Daly's life a rags-to-riches story, but to do so would be an incomplete description of his remarkable life and legacy. Daly did come to America as a poor Irish immigrant, and over the course of his life, he became successful and prosperous. However, it is not his financial success that defines his life; instead, it is what he did with his wealth. Daly's life is the true expression of the American Dream as envisioned by James Truslow Adams,* who coined the term in 1931. Adams was trying to make sense of the Great Depression and concluded that America had lost its way by chasing material success rather than treating money as a means to produce value. He described the American Dream as:

> [T]hat dream of a land in which life should be better and richer and fuller for everyone, with opportunity for each according to ability or achievement. It is a difficult dream for the European upper classes to interpret adequately, and too many of us ourselves have grown weary and mistrustful of it. It is not a dream of motor cars and high wages merely, but a dream of social order in which each man and each woman shall be able to attain to the fullest stature of which they are innately capable, and be recognized by others for what they are, regardless of the fortuitous circumstances of birth or position.[1]

Inherent in Adams's conception of the American Dream is an obligation to others, not only the achievements and prosperity that one might attain for oneself or for one's children. Over time, the idea of the American Dream has become more associated with individual prosperity and less with opportunity for others. And while prosperity has increased for some, the gap between America's wealthy and poor has widened, more than doubling between 1989 and 2016.[2] As the wealth gap grew, opportunity for upward economic mobility shrank. Children

---

* Adams's life was a reflection of his vision of the American Dream. Born into wealth, he entered investment banking, becoming a partner in a New York Stock Exchange member firm. Though he was successful, he was determined to leave Wall Street by the time he reached thirty-five years of age or had accumulated $100,000. At age thirty-five, he left the world of finance and set off to become an accomplished writer, receiving the Pulitzer Prize for his 1921 book, *The Founding of New England*. A decade later, he wrote *The Epic of America*, in which he introduced the term, "the American Dream."

born to families at either the top or the bottom of the economic ladder are likely to remain in similar economic circumstances to which they were born.[3] The result is that fewer American children reach a higher standard of living than their parents, leading many to suggest that the American Dream is dead or greatly diminished.[4]

Harvard economist and MacArthur genius award winner Raj Chetty and his colleagues took a close look at the state of the American Dream with their analysis of upward mobility. Using tax and census records to track data for millions of Americans back to the neighborhoods where they grew up, their research shows that about 90 percent of the children born in 1940 were financially better off than their parents, while only about 50 percent of those born in 1980 would reach that mark.[5] Chetty and his team created a web-based tool, the *Opportunity Atlas*,[6] a colorful map of the United States showing the surprising degree to which people's future prospects depend on where they grow up. Using the web-based tool, one can enter a location, a census tract, or a county and see the results for children who grew up in that place. When it comes to educational level, future income, and other factors, it turns out that *place matters*: some places do better for their children than others. One of the places that does especially well for all children, regardless of the circumstances to which they were born, is Lake County.

The families of Lake County are not particularly wealthy, but the children from families of all income levels do very well. At higher rates than almost anywhere else in the country, Lake County kids stay in school. They graduate from high school on time and go on to college and successful careers. Of the Lakeview students who began high school in 2015, 92 percent graduated on time in 2019, considerably better than the state average of 79 percent.[7] And, according to the *Opportunity Atlas*, 44 percent of the children born in Lake County graduate from college, putting Lake County in the eighty-ninth percentile nationally. The national percentile rate is even higher for Lake County children born into low-income families.* Low-income Lake County kids also beat national averages for future household income as the percentage of children from families in the lowest 20 percent of household income who, as adults, move to the highest 20 percent is among the highest in the country. It is clear that the American Dream is alive and well in Lake County, regardless of the circumstances of one's

---

*According to the Opportunity Atlas, 27 percent of Lake County children born into low-income families graduate from college (ninety-second percentile nationally).

birth or position. It is not only greater educational attainment and affluence but, as I learned in interviews, also greater generosity toward the success of others through the creation of scholarships and community service.

It is a remarkable success story that has been hiding in plain sight in remote Lake County for a hundred years. Other than those who live in Lake County, few have known about the long-term impact of the scholarship. Most of the evidence of the scholarship's impact is scattered around the country in all of the places where its recipients have moved. As our survey showed, most recipients move away from Lake County as their education prepared them for jobs that are simply not available at home. Over time, others move into Lake County, where their children benefit from the many available scholarships and, as those before, move on to new places. Lake County has become an American Dream machine, moving youth from modest circumstances to extraordinarily successful lives.

Almost a century after the Daly scholarship was first awarded, other place-based scholarships are being established all around the country, mostly in places that have not been favored by geography or circumstances. The most well-known of these modern-day programs, the Kalamazoo Promise, [8] was funded by anonymous donors in 2005 for graduates of Kalamazoo high schools. Since then, hundreds of similar programs have been created, all offering the promise of funding for college.[9] These programs differ in the amount of funding offered, the academic requirements, and the colleges recipients may attend, but the programs are alike in that the scholarship is only available to those who live in a specific place: a city, a county, or neighborhood. All of these place-based scholarships engender a promise—the expectation that if one lives in the place covered by the scholarship (and meets other requirements), one will receive support to attend college. As such, they are often called promise programs.[10] The promise matters; if kids know there is a strong likelihood that they'll receive funding for college, most will prepare themselves for that possibility. And as the hundred-year experience of the Daly scholarship has shown—it works.

The impact of the Daly scholarship reaches well beyond the recipients themselves, impacting their children and a much larger community. In 2009, when Charles Bogner (LHS 1935) passed away, his children were puzzled by a bequest in their father's will in which he left $250,000 to the Daly Fund in Lakeview, Oregon. His children, Karen DelAngelo and Charles Bogner Jr., had never heard of the Daly Fund and had only a vague sense of where Lakeview was. They knew their father was born in a small northern California ranching

Charles Bogner at OSC in 1939. (Courtesy of Bogner family)

community, just south of the Oregon border, but did not know much else about his childhood. They knew that their father's parents divorced when he was about seven, and his dad, their grandfather, who was a ranch manager at the ZX Ranch,* arranged for Charles and his sister to be raised by George and Hattie Stombaugh in Lakeview. They also knew he worked as a soda jerk for Burt Snyder at Snyder and Howard's Pharmacy and, after receiving a scholarship, went to OSU. After college, he joined the army and served in Africa and Europe, earning the Bronze Star. They knew much more about their father's life after the military, when he had a successful second career with Teledyne Ryan Aeronautics.

---

*The ZX Ranch, based in Paisley, was founded in the 1880s by a prospector, J.D. Coughlin, who had acquired land through Oregon's Wetlands Act. The ranch changed hands and grew to be one of America's largest cattle operations. When Charles Bogner's father worked on the ranch during the Depression, it included more than 200,000 acres and leased an additional 1.5 million acres. Bob Welch, "The ZX Ranch: The Story behind the Iconic Brand," *American Cowboy*, May 2017.

Wanting to know more about their dad's childhood, Karen and Charles Jr. attended the 2010 Daly Days celebration in Lakeview. After returning to her California home, Karen wrote a thank you note to the Daly Fund trustees:

> I sat down to write a thank you note to you and all the lovely people who shared Daly Days with us, but I found myself trying to make sense of the early life of my dad that was previously unfamiliar to me.
>
> I now see a much clearer picture of my father. I see where he learned to fix anything that runs and he could do it with bubble gum and cotter pins if necessary. I see the wide open fields where he learned to drive any farm equipment or ride a horse. I see the farm land where he learned to grow the best tomatoes on any Army post we set foot upon. I see why he loved his summers working for the forest service alone in a look-out tower. And being alone was never a problem for him. I see why the forest service was a natural career choice for him instead of the mill. I see how he survived 'camping out' in the war all over Africa and Europe for three years. I see why he wanted to go deer hunting and bring back venison for dinner, which none of us could appreciate. I see why he never complained about a lack of anything. He just went out and made lemonade from the lemons life dealt him.
>
> I just kept thinking on Saturday night how much you all would have loved him. He was definitely one of yours. You raised him, educated him and sent him off to replicate your values and lifestyle in the big world.
>
> After this weekend, I totally understand where his emphasis on education was born.[11]

ACKNOWLEDGMENTS

There is a certain symmetry to it all. A conversation with a colleague, Dan Dunham, at the start of my OSU career was the beginning. After retirement, some forty years later, I'm just now finishing this book. Actually, it didn't start off as a book project, but after visits to Lakeview and conversations with Jim Lynch and others, I was hooked. Then, in 2015, I was able to enlist the help of Jordan Hensley, a talented policy studies graduate student. Starting with the list of recipients, we began searching for them. It was slow going at first as most had moved far from Lake County. Jordan suggested we form a Facebook group and encourage people to share the page with family and friends. It worked. Slowly the numbers grew, then with the help of Mark Koenig, the Oregon State University and University of Oregon foundations cross-referenced our list of recipients with their alumni lists, and we were on our way.

We had a great response to the survey, and the results showed tremendous educational and economic impact. By that time I had started interviewing recipients and realized there was much more to the story. I remember telling Jim Lynch that I wanted to write a book about the scholarship. He was encouraging and told me he always hoped someone would write a book that was not only about the scholarship, but also about Bernard Daly. I've tried to do just that and could not have done so without the help of a great many people. Beginning with my first trip to Lakeview a decade ago, many have generously shared their stories and encouraged me in my writing. Quite literally, this book would not exist without their support. I apologize for not acknowledging every conversation and email communication; each and every one helped.

The power of a promise is central to the story of the Daly scholarship, and it was through Connie Robertson that I first began to understand the power of the promise that Daly made to Connie and all Lake County youth. Connie's niece, Janice (Decker) Kniskern, told me about her aunt (and her mother, Joycelyn), and shared letters that Connie wrote while in college. In our conversation, Janice also told me that there was someone from Lakeview who had done something with NASA, and I should try to find him. It took a while, but I did find Gene Peterson; at ninety-nine, he was my oldest interviewee. It was through Gene and others that I learned how the scholarship impacted more than just the recipients. The Daly scholarship was, and still is, the rising tide that raises all boats.

That's how it worked; one conversation led to another, and another. In a Skype call with Jean Tesche, who was working in South Africa at the time, Jean said I should take a look at the class of 1961 as she thought it was quite exceptional. When Jean was in high school, she loved languages and learned Russian after school from a 1961 graduate, Marion Angele, Gene Peterson's niece. I followed up on Jean's suggestion and interviewed Marion and other '61 graduates: Jim Clinton, Arpad Kovacsy, Gail (Robin) Clinton, Lawrence Decker, and Ted Conn's son, Ken Conn. It was a talented graduation class, but there were many others.

I can't remember who told me to look up John Horne, but I'm glad I did. John told me that I should talk with Shelley Means and Linda Williams. It was as though the chapters were assembling themselves through the people I talked with. There were times when it seemed I talked or corresponded with someone from Lake County every day. There was the day when I was at the OSU recreation center and a man came up to me and asked, "Are you the guy doing research on the Daly scholarship?" That was Craig Creel. Craig and his sister, Lou Creel, and Barbara Lee, among others, introduced me to King Lee. I've heard so many stories about King's Café, I can almost taste the egg foo young.

I met many families, often interviewing parents, grandparents, brothers, and sisters, all of whom received either the Daly or the Collins McDonald scholarship. I remember sitting in Barb Simpson's living room writing as fast as I could, trying to keep up with Bill Barry as he told me about each of his kids and what they were doing—all were Daly recipients. I interviewed three generations of the Howard family, probably the most conversation I've ever had with pharmacists. I'm especially grateful to the Ogle family. They, along with Dan Dunham and Jim Lynch, were my introduction to the scholarship and the larger Lake County community. I still remember the LP record–size pancakes at the community ranch breakfast that Jim Ogle and Dorothy (Withers) Ogle hosted. I am especially grateful to their daughter, Sue (Ogle) Densmore, who invited me to the breakfast and steadily encouraged my research efforts.

Jim Lynch and his extended family have been with me every step of the way. Through Jim, I met his wife, Eleanor, who patiently answered questions when Jim no longer could and introduced me to her daughter, Christine (Verges) Gacharna. In addition to telling me about Jim and her classmates, Christine encouraged me to talk with David Maxey, who had worked on the Lynch ranch with Jim. David's memories of the ranch, Jim, and Lake County have been an inspiration for me. David connected me with Jim's sister, Breda (Lynch) Flynn, who helped me track the Lynch family back to Ireland.

As a longtime educator, I especially enjoyed meeting Lake County teachers and administrators. I interviewed four Lake County school superintendents: Howard Ottman, Sean Gallagher, Will Cahill, and Michael Carter. In addition to describing the schools, Will Cahill took me on a tour of Adel, complete with lunch at the Adel store and a ride over Fandango Pass. As you might expect, teachers were especially helpful in my search for information about former students. Lake County has been fortunate to have had so many talented teachers who went the extra distance for their students.

Many of the English teachers I met were particularly helpful since they had grown up in Lakeview: Sharon (Washburn) Faulkner, Barb Simpson, and Lisa (Warner) Shullanberger. I feel a connection with Lakeview students as I, too, had my writing improved by Barb Simpson, who reviewed early drafts of the book. My interviews with science and math teachers Chris (Radford) Hill, Clair Thomas, Randy Bell, Ty Tuchscherer, Noni Vandenberg, and Mark Louie showed me how they connected their teaching with the real world through creative outside-of-school activities.

Along the way, I benefitted greatly from the research and writing of others. I couldn't possibly mention them all, but here are a few that were especially helpful. Hidetaka Hirota's research on the exclusion of poor Irish through state passenger laws helped me solve the mystery of why Bernard Daly and his family emigrated to Selma, Alabama, during the Civil War. David Gleeson, author of *The Irish in the South: 1815–1877*, took the time to correspond with me about the Irish population in Selma during the Civil War. Marie Kelleher's wonderful book *Duhallow to Oregon* tells the story of the micro-migration from Duhallow, Ireland, to Lake County and the early years of sheepherding in Lake County. Lake County historian Melany Tupper's in-depth investigation of Creed Conn's death sheds new light on a century-old murder mystery. The research of Raj Chetty and the Opportunity Insights group provided the data that showed the remarkable educational and economic impact of the Daly scholarship on those who moved away from Lake County.

Tracing the life of Bernard Daly was like trying to do a jigsaw puzzle without the pieces. Thanks to the help of university archives, genealogical records,

Lake County Courthouse records, the Lake County Museum, and the correspondence between Daly and Pearl Hall, I was able to find some of the pieces. Piece by piece, Bernard Daly came to life. Ohio Northern and the University of Louisville archives shared Daly's college records and artifacts of campus life during his student days. I am especially grateful to Larry Landis, former director of the OSU Archives. Larry and his staff helped me locate many materials, including records of the Oregon Agricultural College Regents when Bernard Daly was a member. Larry also helped arrange for me to borrow the Pearl Hall papers from the University of Oregon Archives. It was through Daly's letters to Pearl that I could hear his voice and feel his manner. I'm deeply grateful to Eleanor Lynch. who told her husband, Jim, that he should get those letters out of the basement of his law office to a place where others could access them.

I am especially glad that this book is being published by the OSU Press with editing by Cheryl McLean of Imprint Services, and in collaboration with the Dr. Daly Project Association. It's a dream team for me, given my long relationship with OSU and the book's alignment with the Dr. Daly Project's mission of promoting awareness of Bernard Daly and his scholarship.

Above all, I am grateful for the support of my friends and family. They listened to story after story and still remained steadfast in their support of me and their belief in the book. Extra special thanks to Beth, my partner in all things.

NOTES

Introduction
[1] Helen L. Mershon, "A Proud Legacy: Lake County Scholars Assisted by Daly Fund," *Oregon Journal*, October 1979.

Chapter 1
[1] John Kelly, *The Graves Are Walking* (New York, NY: Henry Holt and Company, 2012).

[2] Hidetaka Hirota, *Expelling the Poor: Atlantic Seaboard States and the Nineteenth-Century Origins of American Immigration Policy* (New York: Oxford University Press, 2017).

[3] David T. Gleeson, *The Irish in the South, 1815–1877* (Chapel Hill: University of North Carolina Press, 2002).

[4] Pearl Hall, "Pearl Hall Collection of Bernard Daly Material, 1897–1943."

[5] Sarah Lehr Kennedy, *H. S. Lehr and His School: A Story of the Private Normal Schools* (Ada, OH: Ada Herald, 1938).

[6] Paul Logsdon, "A Pictorial History of Ohio Northern University" (Ada, OH: Ohio Northern University, 2008), https://my.onu.edu/files/Pictorial_History_of_Ohio_Northern_University.pdf.

[7] Pearl Hall Collection.

[8] Kennedy, *H. S. Lehr and His School.*

[9] Ohio Normal University, "Thirteenth Annual Commencement of the Ohio Normal University" (Ada, OH: Ohio Normal University, 1886).

[10] "Alumni News," *Ohio Normal University Herald*, August 23, 1886.

[11] Hampden C. Lawson, "The Early Medical Schools of Kentucky," *Bulletin of the History of Medicine* 24, no. 2 (1950): 168–75.

[12] Lawson, "The Early Medical Schools of Kentucky."

[13] Andrew H. Beck, "The Flexner Report and the Standardization of American Medical Education," *Journal of the American Medical Association* 291, no. 17 (2004): 2139–40.

[14] Abraham Flexner, *The American College: A Criticism* (New York: The Century Co., 1908).

[15] Malcolm Cox et al., "American Medical Education 100 Years After the Flexner Report," *New England Journal of Medicine* 355, no. 13 (2006): 1339–44, https://doi.org/https://doi.org/10.1056/NEJMra055445.

[16] Abraham Flexner, *Medical Education in the United States and Canada*, The Carnegie Foundation for the Advancement of Teaching, Bulletin Number Four, 1910, http://archive.carnegiefoundation.org/publications/medical-education-united-states-and-canada-bulletin-number-four-flexner-report.html.

Chapter 2

[1] Pearl Hall, "Interview with Mr. Light," 1939. Pearl Hall Collection.

[2] T. D. Snyder, "120 Years of American Education: A Statistical Portrait," *Statistics*, 1993, http://nces.ed.gov/pubs93/93442.pdf.

[3] William G. Robbins, *The People's School: A History of Oregon State University* (Corvallis: Oregon State University Press, 2017).

[4] Robbins, *The People's School.*

[5] Edward Gardner Jones, ed., *The Oregonian's Handbook of the Pacific Northwest* (The Oregonian Publishing Company, 1894).

[6] Oregon Secretary of State, Journal of the House of the Legislative Assembly of the State of Oregon for the Seventeenth Regular Session 1893 (Salem, OR: Frank C. Baker, State Printer, 1893), https://babel.hathitrust.org/cgi/pt?id=nyp.33433019341530&view=1up&seq=11.

[7] "Dr. Bernard Daly Dies," *Lake County Examiner*, January 8, 1920.

[8] Phil F. Brogan, *East of the Cascades*, ed. L. K. Phillips (Portland, OR: Binford & Mort Publishers, 1964).

[9] Hall, "Interview with Mr. Light."

[10] O. K. Burrell, *Gold in the Woodpile: An Informal History of Banking in Oregon* (Eugene, OR: University of Oregon Press, 1967).

[11] Melva Bach, "History of the Fremont National Forest" (Lakeview, OR: Fremont National Forest, 1981).

[12] Journal of the Senate of the Tenth Regular Session of the Legislative Assembly of Oregon (Salem, OR: W. B. Carter, State Printer, 1878), https://catalog.hathitrust.org/Record/008607921, https://catalog.hathitrust.org/Record/008607921.

[13] "Reapportionment Bill," *Oregonian*, 1899.

Chapter 3

[1] Editorial, "No," *Oregonian*, June 12, 1896.

[2] "Daly Is for Silver," *Oregonian*, May 13, 1900.

[3] "Returns to Lakeview," *Oregonian*, May 27, 1900.

[4] "Politics in Lake County," *Oregonian*, May 17, 1900.

[5] Bernard Daly to Pearl Hall, 1900, Pearl Hall Collection.

[6] Georgie Ellen Boydstun Stephenson, *The Growth of Lake County, Oregon* (Wilsonville, OR: BookPartners, 1994).

[7] Pearl Hall Collection.

[8] Pearl Hall Collection.

[9] Bernard Daly to Pearl Hall, 1904, Pearl Hall Collection.

[10] Melany Tupper, *The Sandy Knoll Murder: Legacy of the Seepshooters* (Christmas Valley, OR: Central Oregon Books, 2010).

[11] Pearl Hall to Bernard Daly, 1909, Pearl Hall Collection.

[12] "Unblushing Land Frauds," *New York Times*, March 20, 1888.

[13] "One Land Grant Less in Oregon," *Oregonian*, September 26, 1909.

[14] Stephenson, *The Growth of Lake County, Oregon*.

[15] Bernard Daly to Pearl Hall, 1909, Pearl Hall Collection.

[16] Lake County Historical Society, *Lake County History: The First 100 Years* (Bend, OR: Maverick Publications, 2008).

[17] Eric Hilt and Wendy M. Rahn, "Turning Citizens into Investors: Promoting Savings with Liberty Bonds During World War I," *The Russell Sage Foundation Journal of the Social Sciences* 2, no. 6 (2016): 86–108.

[18] "Lake Going Strong," *Oregonian*, April 21, 1918.

Chapter 4

[1] Hall, "Interview with Mr. Light."

[2] Typed copy of an article in the *Lakeview Herald*, October 27, 1910. Pearl Hall Collection.

[3] Bernard Daly Will, 1919.

[4] University of Oregon Catalogue 1922–1923 (Eugene, OR, 1922).

[5] "Lake Students Win Gift of $800,000," *Oregonian*, 1921.

[6] Connie Robertson to Joycelin Robertson, 1922.

[7] Connie Robertson to Juno Robertson, 1923.

[8] "Virgil Woodcock, Ex-Head of Patent Law Association," *New York Times*, June 2, 1974.

[9] Clarence Boyer and George Peavy to Daly Fund Trustees, 1937.

[10] Claudia Goldin, "America's Graduation from High School: The Evolution and Spread of Secondary Schooling in the Twentieth Century," *Journal of Economic History* 58, no. 2 (1998): 345–74.

Chapter 5

[1] Jim Ogle, *Powell and Ogle Family Story*, 2018.

[2] Edwin Kiester, "The GI Bill May Be the Best Deal Ever Made by Uncle Sam," *Smithsonian* 25, no. 8 (1994): 128–37.

[3] Peter F. Drucker, *Post-Capitalist Society* (New York: HarperBusiness, 1994).

[4] Douglas Perry, "Oregon WWI Vet Led 20,000-Strong Bonus Army in 1932 That Marched on Nation's Capital, Met Brutal Resistance," *Oregonian*, August 14, 2020, https://www.oregonlive.com/history/2020/08/oregon-wwi-vet-led-20000-strong-bonus-army-in-1932-that-marched-on-nations-capital-met-brutal-resistance.html.

[5] Lake County Historical Society, *Lake County History: The First 100 Years* (Bend, OR: Maverick Publications, 2008).

[6] Jim Ogle and Clayton Chocktoot, *Fort Rock and Paisley Cave Descendants* (Lakeview, OR: Lake County Historical Society, 2018).

[7] Marie Kelleher, *Duhallow to Oregon 1880–1960* (Kanturk, Ireland: Kanturk Printers Ltd., 1985).

Chapter 6

[1] Christian Trejbal, "From Community Activist To Longtime Mayor," *The Source Weekly*, Bend, Oregon, August 31, 2016.

[2] John R. Thelin, *Going to College in the Sixties* (Baltimore: Johns Hopkins University Press, 2018).

[3] Vince Patton, "Agent Orange Dump Site Is Oregon Desert's Toxic Legacy," Salem-News.com, May 7, 2012, http://www.salem-news.com/articles/may072012/oregon-agent-orange-vp.php .

[4] Wallace Turner, "Lumber Industry Woes Dim Good Life in Oregon," *New York Times*, March 3, 1982, https://www.nytimes.com/1982/03/03/us/lumber-industry-woes-dim-good-life-in-oregon.html.

[5] Lake County Historical Society, *Lake County History: The First 100 Years*, 91–92

[6] Lake County Historical Society, *Lake County History*.

Chapter 7

[1] Tom Kloster, "Exploring Mitchell Point," *WyEast* (blog), 2021,
https://wyeastblog.org/2012/05/05/exploring-mitchell-point.
Oregon Department of Transportation, "Historic Columbia River Highway," n.d.

[2] Alicia Andrews and Kristin Kutara, "Oregon's Timber Harvests: 1849–2004"
(Salem, OR: Oregon Department of Forestry, 2005), https://www.oregon.gov/
ODF/Documents/WorkingForests/oregonstimberharvests.pdf.

[3] Alicia Ault, "Medicine Creek, the Treaty That Set the Stage for Standing Rock,"
Smithsonian (Washington, DC, June 2017), https://www.smithsonianmag.com/
smithsonian-institution/standing-rock-there-was-medicine-creek-180963623.

[4] Bill Richards, "Silicon Forest: For Oregon, the Boom In High Tech Brings Jobs and
Handwringing," *Wall Street Journal*, August 4, 1995. Gordon B. Dodds and Craig
E. Wollner, *Silicon Forest: High Tech in the Portland Area 1945–1986* (Portland:
Oregon Historical Society Press, 1990).

[5] Susan P. Choy and Xiaojie Li, "Debt Burden: A Comparison of 1992–1993 and
1999–2000 Bachelor's Degree Recipients a Year After Graduating" (Washington,
DC: US Department of Education, National Center for Education Statistics, 2005),
https://nces.ed.gov/pubs2005/2005170.pdf.

[6] Laura Singer et al., "Lakeview, Oregon: The Little Town That Collaboration Saved"
(Portland, OR, 2011), https://pdxscholar.library.pdx.edu/ncpp_pub/15. Greg
Hanscom, "A Timber Town Learns to Care for the Forest," *High Country News*,
September 27, 2004, https://hcn.org/issues/283/15022. Brandi Larson,
"Chewaucan Biophysical Monitoring Team: Local Kids Make a Big Impact in
Forestry Management," *High Country News*, 2016.

Chapter 8

[1] Kristen Bialik and Richard Fry, "Millennial Life: How Young Adulthood
Today Compares with Prior Generations" (Washington, DC: Pew Research
Center, 2020), https://www.pewresearch.org/social-trends/2019/02/14/
millennial-life-how-young-adulthood-today-compares-with-prior-generations-2.

[2] Jimmy Hall, "Lakeview Artist Exhibits in the Big Apple," *Lake County Examiner*,
September 14, 2016.

[3] Sylva Florence, "Ladies Can't What?," *The Sylva Lining* (blog), 2018.

[4] Sylva Florence, "Presenting Roads Less Traveled," *The Sylva Lining* (blog), 2018.

[5] Sylva Florence, "A Florence in the Forest (And It's Been A Long Time Coming),"
The Sylva Lining (blog), 2020.

[6] Sarah D. Sparks, "Calculus Is the Peak of High School Math. Maybe It's Time to Change That," *Education Week*, May 2018, https://www.edweek.org/teaching-learning/calculus-is-the-peak- of-high-school-math-maybe-its-time-to-change-that/2018/05.

Epilogue

[1] James Truslow Adams, ed., *The Epic of America* (Boston: Little, Brown and Company, 1931).

[2] Katherine Schaeffer, "6 Facts about Economic Inequality in the U.S.," Pew Research Center FACT TANK: News in the Numbers, February 7, 2020, https://www.pewresearch.org/fact-tank/2020/02/07/6-facts-about-economic-inequality-in-the-u-s.

[3] Pablo A. Mitnik and David B. Grusky, "Economic Mobility in the United States" (Philadelphia, 2015), https://www.pewtrusts.org/~/media/assets/2015/07/fsm-irs-report_artfinal.pdf.

[4] Carol Graham, "Is the American Dream Really Dead," *Guardian*, June 20, 2017, https://www.theguardian.com/inequality/2017/jun/20/is-the-american-dream-really-dead.

[5] Raj Chetty et al., "The Fading American Dream: Trands in Absolute Income Mobility Since 1940" (Cambridge, MA: National Bureau of Economic Research, December 2016), https://opportunityinsights.org/wp-content/uploads/2018/03/abs_mobility_paper.pdf.

[6] https://www.opportunityatlas.org.

[7] Oregon Department of Education, "Lake County School District 2019–20 Profile," *At-A-Glance School and District Profiles*, 2020, https://www.oregon.gov/ode/schools-and-districts/reportcards/reportcards/Documents/Adapted1920/1920-AAAG-2059.pdf.

[8] https://www.kalamazoopromise.com.

[9] https://www.collegepromise.org.

[10] Michelle Miller-Adams, Promise Nation: Transforming Communities through Place-Based Scholarships, W.E. Upjohn Institute for Employment Research, 2015, https://research.upjohn.org/cgi/viewcontent.cgi?article=1253&context=up_press.

[11] Karen DelAngelo to Daly Fund Trustees, 2010.

INDEX